PILGRIMS AND PURITANS IN COLONIAL AMERICA

PILGRIMS AND PURITANS IN COLONIAL AMERICA

Regulatory Laws
in the New England Colonies,
1630-1686

LIEVIN KAMBAMBA MBOMA

NASHVILLE, TN

Front Cover:
Title: Gov. John Winthrop -- In honor of the birthday of Governor John Winthrop, born June 12, 1587 / K. H. Burn del.
Date Created/Published: [between 1860 and 1880]
Medium: 1 print: wood engraving.
Summary: Head-and-shoulders portrait of Gov. John Winthrop, flanked by statues of a Native American (left) and a pilgrim (right).
Reproduction Number: LC-USZ62-120506 (b&w film copy neg.)
Rights Advisory: No known restrictions on publication.
Call Number: BIOG FILE - Winthrop, John, 1588-1649 <item> [P&P]
Repository: Library of Congress Prints and Photographs Division Washington, D.C. 20540 USA

Back Cover:
The pilgrims signing the compact, on board the May Flower, Nov. 11th, 1620 / painted by T.H. Matteson; engraved by Gauthier.
- Entered according to Act of Congress in the year 1859 by W. Schaus, in the Clerk's Office of the District Court of the United States for the southern District of New-York.
- A key to this print is in LOT 11507.
No known restrictions on publication.

Contents

Acknowledgements

During my research and the writing of book manuscripts, I have received enormous support, suggestions, and guidance from scholars such as Professors Jan Vansina, former history professor at the University of Wisconsin, Madison; John K. Thornton, history professor at Boston University in Boston; William M. Marvin, former history professor and chair of the University of Texas at Arlington history department; Adebayo Oyebade, history professor and chair at the department of history at Tennessee State University; Bobby Lovett, former Dean and history professor at Tennessee State University; Jewell Parham, professor of African American literature; Dr. Tom Kanon, former archivist at Tennessee State Archives; and Professor Daniel Sharfstein at the Vanderbilt Law School and the Department of History. These scholars have shaped my research skills and analysis. For that reason, I credit their contributions on my work.

In addition to the listed scholars, Kirkus Production Editor Stephanie Summerhays deserves credit for guiding me during the editing process of this work. My additional thanks to Kirsten B. for editing this book with special attention. In addition to the Kirkus editors, I am grateful to Lisa Borre, Testing Center Manager at Volunteer State Community College, for proofreading the manuscript during the final stage. Her contribution is worth noting. Moreover, I acknowledge the input of Dr. Raymond Kinzounza, Branch Manager at Pruitt Public Library in Nashville. He read the entire manuscript before its submission to the Kirkus Magazine Reviews. Furthermore, I also appreciate the contribution of Kelley Sirca, Program Coordinator at the Nashville Metro Archive, for her contributions to my work.

Finally, I also credit my family and friends for giving me moral support during the long process of my work, especially, Bradlee Wilson; Grace May; Joseph Nwankwo, Attorney at Law in Nashville,

Tennessee; Alfred Yaba, Luseni Kromah, Sallue Kromah, Peter Edobar
and Chryso Kasongo Kahambwe.

Regarding this work, I take full responsibility for the data collection, analysis, and interpretation. The listed scholars do not bear any
responsibility in this work.

Preface

In 2013, while I was collecting data for my book *African Descendants in Colonial America: Impact on the Preservation of Peace, Security, and Safety in New England, 1638–1783*, I was surprised to discover regulatory laws enforced in colonial New England that are parallel to those of the United States. For that reason, many questions came into my mind. Is it due to these colonial regulatory features that colonial New England was well-regulated? Was the economic development of the New England colonies due to the observation of the rule of law and regulatory folkways from their forefathers? How did the colonists observe the same regulatory culture for centuries, with few modifications, as their forefathers had in England? These questions would not be explained without an investigation. They can be understood only after a careful examination of laws observed for regulatory purposes in colonial New England. Furthermore, the way in which the colonists approved and obeyed regulatory laws in New England was impressive to me. During the colonial era, officials regulated the behaviors of their subjects according to the established laws. As a result, every citizen in the colony was familiarized with the norms and laws of the society in which they resided.

In the same region, the division of power and local self-control were maintained as the laws of each colony demanded. Importantly, among the colonies in colonial New England, laws were somewhat very similar. Therefore, how did this legal uniformity arise in the first place? Like other questions, the commonality of regulatory laws in New England will be detailed after a careful review of how the colonies were settled.

New England's regulatory laws have been noted by many historians and also by the United States Department of Labor. Alden Bradford, in his book *History of Massachusetts for Two Hundred Years: From the Year*

1620 to 1820, noted how the laws of the colony were prepared. According to him, the character of the inhabitants and the conditions of the colony were considered before the laws were enacted. He also listed many regulatory laws pertaining to schools and the compensation of governors. Like Bradford, Charles Patrick Neill also noted many school regulations in Massachusetts. Furthermore, in *The Charters and General Laws of the Colony and Province of Massachusetts Bay,* regulatory laws for the managing of servants, local officials' salaries, and government institutions were discussed. Regulatory laws were also detailed in *The Laws and Liberties of Massachusetts.* Massachusetts' regulatory laws were also mentioned by Joseph Barlow Felt in his book *An Historical Account of Massachusetts Currency.* Like Felt, Alonzo Lewis discussed price regulations in Massachusetts. Moreover, Lewis commented on the self-governing power entrusted to each town in the same colony. In his book *The History of Lynn,* he emphasized the salaries of teachers and the control of wages for laborers. Similar regulatory laws were posited by Caleb Hopkins Snow in his book *A History of Boston, the Metropolis of Massachusetts, from Its Origin to the Present Period; with Some Account of the Environs.* In this work, Snow detailed the minimum wage set forth by the government for workers. Like Felt, Snow elucidated the salary of local officials in Massachusetts. The Boston historian Samuel Gardner Drake recorded authoritative data on the regulatory laws of Massachusetts. In his work, he detailed the regulation of ferries and the power entrusted to the marshal for the same regulatory purposes. In the same colony, Drake noted the consequences reserved for employers who violated the minimum wage regulations set for laborers such as carpenters and other laborers. He discussed the post office regulation as well as the location where the post office was situated. Drake also pointed out the process of handling and delivering mail according to regulatory laws set forth by the General Court of Massachusetts. In addition to the authors listed previously, Alice Morse Earle's book *Customs and Fashions in Old New England* adds important information on the manner in which the conduct of the inhabitants was regulated. It is sound to note that the success of colonial leaders in enforcing their laws depended on how the inhabitants' behavior was managed. With the observation of religious laws, settlers and other community members were obligated to live a Christian life. Those who deviated from such order were punished accordingly. Colonists introduced working culture to children early in their lives. Likewise, religious teaching took the same pace. Laws enacted for the regulation of children were discussed by Charles Patrick Neill in his *book Summary of the Report on Condition of Woman and Child Wage Earners in the United States*, published in 1915. In his *New England Journal*, Governor John Winthrop mentioned regulatory laws observed in the Massachusetts Bay Colony. William Bradford's *History of Plymouth Plantation* reveals significant data on the migration of people from Massachusetts Bay to the Connecticut River.

In Rhode Island, the regulatory laws of the colony can be found in *The Records of the Colony of Rhode Island and Providence Plantations, in New England, 1741–1756*. In this document, the wages of military men and local officials were also mentioned. Regulatory laws of the same colony can be found in the work of William B. Weeden in his book *Economic and Social History of New England 1620–1789*. Weeden's work remains a prominent historical account of the colonial New England economy. He is one of the first authors to tackle the economy and the social history of New England from the colonial period to the early republic.

In Connecticut, a local historian named Benjamin Trumbull collected well-documented data on the annual salary of the governor. In the same context, *The Public Records of the Colony of Connecticut [1636–1776]* revealed regulatory laws enacted in that colony for the protection of workers. In these documents, the regulations of ferries and the respective salaries of the governors and county officials were detailed. As early as 1630, New England colonists established humane regulatory laws that were observed and executed for the management of the daily affairs of the government at each level. It is likely, then, that the behaviors of the inhabitants in the colonies were regulated by the laws colonial officials enacted.

Contrary to the works written by the authors listed previously, this current academic work is interdisciplinary in its nature. Many topics are discussed separately, and references to Germany and England are incorporated. In this current book, a brief history of Germanic tribes and their migrations to England is noted. Similarly, the invasion of England by the Danes is discussed. Regarding regulatory laws, the acts observed in England for the establishment and management of schools are illustrated to indicate the continuation of this culture in the New England colonies and its subsequent use by Anglo-Americans. Like school regulations, wages and prices are also discussed with reference to the laws of England. The codifications of laws are also discussed.

Pertaining to the works written by the authors listed previously, Weeden's contribution is unique for its merits and content. But he failed to discuss the enactment and enforcement of New England's regulatory laws for the management and establishment of schools. Moreover, in his various discussions, he lumped together regulatory laws for wages and price controls. On the contrary, in this current work, the author will examine these topics separately to ensure each gets its fair share of attention.

Introduction

New England's regulatory laws have been discussed by numerous scholars and historians for many years preceding my work. Among these historians, the work of William B. Weeden remains the most notable. His work—*Economic and Social History of New England, 1620–1789*—has been a touchstone for scholars in this field. In his books, he details the regulatory laws of various cities in the colony of Massachusetts.[1] Such laws were recorded in colonial records and provincial papers. To illustrate, in *Provincial Papers. Documents and Records Relating to the Province of New Hampshire, from the Earliest Period of Its Settlement*, many of the colony's regulatory laws were mentioned. Nathaniel Bouton, the compiler of that document, recorded important information on the colony, such as the names of governors, its laws, the post office, wage regulations, and price controls.[2] In like manner, many New England historical societies hold colonial laws. Moreover, in *The Charter and Laws of the Colony and Province of Massachusetts Bay*, regulatory laws of that colony are discussed.

In the *Collection of the Massachusetts Historical Society*, many regulatory laws for that colony are recorded, including the authoritatively detailed regulations regarding the management of the post office in New England. Regulations covering missing letters, restrictions, rates, and duties of the postmaster general were noted.[3] Regarding regulation of prices, *The History of New England from 1630 to 1649, Volume 2* by Governor John Winthrop is one of the best documents to consult while conducting research on regulatory laws in colonial Massachusetts. In this book, Winthrop related authoritative data on the administration of the colony. He noted the duties of the governor and the power of the general court on controlling the prices of domestic products. Furthermore, he discussed the daily wages of employees and the consequences reserved to those who violated the colony's regulatory laws regarding wages. Moreover, he elucidated the difficulties the colony faced while regulating wages. Due to those handicaps, the general court empowered local officials to regulate wages in their respective towns. He also posited the enactment of the Body of Liberties.[4] In this legal corpus, many regulatory laws were also listed. Regulatory laws in the Body of Liberties will be discussed in chapter 5.

Like the earlier historian, modern historians and scholars have also investigated colonial regulatory laws, especially those covering colonial wages. Even though such works exist, many historians believe there is insufficient interest of various scholars in that matter. To illustrate, the compiler of *The History of Wages in the United States from Colonial Time to 1828, Vol. 53*, who was employed at the United States Bureau of Labor, lamented that the study of colonial wages has always been overlooked by most American historians.[5] In his work, the compiler of this history credited William B. Weeden and Philip A. Bruce for tackling the regulation of wages during the colonial era. According to the work completed at the United States Bureau of Labor, the works of Weeden and Bruce give us the general framework for the matter in question. It appears that both covered the same ground, and data used for the piecing together of their books were collected from secondary data. To cover the missing ground, the compiler of the United States Bureau of Labor collected primary data from the Baker Library of the Harvard Graduate School of Business Administration. In this library, large volumes of regulatory laws in colonial America are recorded. For example, wages paid to employees at the Saugus Iron Works from its beginning to 1643 are recorded. In 1915, Ethelbert Stewart, chief statistician of the United States Department of Labor, wrote an article titled "Bricklayers Wages and Conditions: Colonial to Organization Days." In this work, Stewart also discussed daily wages paid to workers such as bricklayers in the colonies of Massachusetts, Connecticut, and Virginia. He also noted the methods of payment observed in each colony discussed in his article.[6]

After reading the work of historians and an employee of the United States Bureau of Labor, I discovered that other colonial regulatory laws were not covered except wages. Therefore, I decided to add up other areas of regulatory laws that were not discussed by all the authors listed previously. Contrary to the previous work, which covered wages, this current work explores the demographic background of leaders entrusted with making regulatory laws for public conduct, wage controls, price controls, schools, ferry regulations, and the post office. In regard to the post office, in this book I will discuss the rate for the delivery of mails, the restrictions set forth for dispatching mail and packages, the duties of the postmaster, mail's protections, the duties of the postman, and the post locations in each colony. The post office's laws enacted by the general court were also discussed. The areas noted previously were well-regulated for the development of the colonies in New England. Additionally, this book will provide a brief biography of the colonial leaders who were empowered to enact the various laws. Furthermore, I will also discuss how laws were promulgated during the earlier years of the colony before the printing companies were built. In New England, printing companies were not introduced until long after the English had settled the land.

This study of the regulatory laws in the New England colonies is suitable for students, researchers, professors, and scholars focusing on the economic development of that region. Because these early laws were so foundational, studying them is essential to understanding how they shaped subsequent laws.

Chapter 1

The Crown of England
and the Colonization Movement

The impact made by the crowns of England on discoveries, exploitations, and foreign trade is documented by English and American scholars and historians. The accounts of the contributions of the crowns of England regarding the planting of colonies in North America were elucidated by Edward W. McGlenen, Edward O. Skelton, and Edward M. Hartwell. In their work titled *Boston and Its Story, 1630–1915*, these editors noted that "ten years before the publication of Smith's *Description of New England*, the English Crown had adopted the policy of actively promoting the colonization of those parts of North America which it claimed to possess by virtue of the discovery of the Cabot family in 1487 and 1498 under the patronage of Henry the VII."[1] From the account of these American writers, one can stipulate that the crown of England understood the importance of having colonies overseas for both security and commercial reasons.

The writings of Henry Duff Trail, George Bancroft, Richard Biddle, and Patrick Colquhoun revealed that the crowns of England were interested in the improvement of their kingdom's trade. Therefore, discovery, navigation, and exploration of new lands were imperative to them. Like the authors mentioned previously, James Fawckner Nicholls, David Hume, Francesco Tarducci, and Lucy Aikin have discussed the contributions made by the crowns of England on discovery missions. These writers' accounts emphasize how the royal family was devoted to occupying overseas territories, just like the Spanish and Portuguese had. During this period, the kings of Spain and Portugal generated much money from trade conducted by their subjects in the "New World." Perhaps King Henry VII was also motivated for the same reasons, due to his commercial interests. Just like him, his successors, King Henry VIII and Queen Elizabeth, valued commercial transactions executed by their subjects for the interests of the kingdom. English monarchs enforced the security of English sailors as well-maintained diplomatic missions for the interest of the English traders and explorers.

In England, the discovery missions in North America have been accredited to King Henry VII, who supported the exploration of North America by John Cabot and his son Sebastian Cabot. In 1497, the Cabot family, including the Plymouth and Bristol sailors, discovered the New England regions.[2] Francis Bacon, who worked in the court of King Henry and others, stated that King Henry VII procured the men who traveled with Cabot to the northern part of America. He went on to posit that Bristol sailors and London merchants were included in the discovery of the northern regions of America during the voyage of Sebastian Cabot.[3] Like other writers, Richard Johnson articulates that John Cabot discovered Newfoundland in 1497.[4] From the information noted by these authors, it is essential to relate that King Henry's interest in the discovery of the unknown land to the Europeans was one issue of his foreign policy. At this period, the kings of Spain and Portugal were powerful due to the rights of discoveries of new territories overseas. South America belonged to the king of Spain, due to his right to discovery of that land by Christopher Columbus. In like manner, the West Coast of Africa, precisely the Island of Cape Vert, Mandera, the Kingdom of Kongo, Angola, including Guinea, were under the rights of Portugal. In 1482, Diego Coca, a Portuguese subject, arrived at the mouth of the Congo River. As such, this entire territory belonged to the king of Portugal. The kings of Portugal and Spain were prone to mistreat British seamen found in their supposed territories. Therefore, the discovery of Southern Virginia and Northern Virginia was important for the English. The work of John Cabot gives King Henry VII and his descendants, including his subjects, the rights of planting a colony, exploring, and conducting trade in North America without interference from any European powers. In the same context, Spanish kings had the right of South America by right of discovery of that land by Columbus.

English sailors from towns like Bristol, Plymouth, and Exeter were motivated by Cabot. In addition, London merchants were excited for the same purpose. The discovery of Northern Virginia regions by a person related to England through residency was a remarkable accomplishment for the kingdom, especially the London, Plymouth, and Exeter merchants. These merchants were devoted to expanding their trade and making profits. As the northern regions of America were claimed by King Henry VII, his subjects' dreams of planting colonies in the New World became a reality. It is essential to narrate shortly the history of exploration during and before the reign of King Henry VII.

Before the discovery of the northwest region of America by Cabot, King Henry VII was in negotiation with Bartholomew Columbus for the discovery mission of the unknown land. The negotiation between Columbus and King Henry did not go well. It appears that King Henry was not persuaded by Bartholomew Columbus's propositions. According to Henry Duff Trail, in 1484, Bartholomew was dispatched by his brother, Christopher, to England for a discovery mission on the patronage of King Henry VII. But on his way to England, Bartholomew was captured by pirates, who enslaved him for a few months. Upon his escape, he went to England, hoping to accomplish the mission of his brother in the name of the king. When he arrived back in England, Bartholomew was ill and impoverished. In 1488, when Bartholomew met King Henry VII, he carried with him a map of the New World. The king, who was interested in the discovery mission, promised to support him with his design. Contrary to the king's plan, Columbus was impatient and left England.[5]

King Henry VII was a patriotic leader, and he employed every effort for the expansion of commerce and discovery missions to different parts of the world. In 1502, he issued a grant for Hugh Elliot and Thomas Ashurst, both Bristol merchants, and John Gunsolus and Francis Farnandus, natives of Portugal, for discovery missions. They were ordered to procure ships and marines that would enable them to achieve their plans.[6] King Henry VII ordered these sailors to explore the eastern, western, southern, and northern seas in order to discover, recover, and investigate the various islands and sundry countries. The grant stipulated that, upon discovering such lands, they were authorized to erect King Henry's banner. In addition to that, the persons listed previously were obligated to hold the newly claimed lands or territories for the crown. King Henry VII had a plan for any territory discovered by Hugh Elliot's team. According to Adam Anderson, King Henry VII planned the construction of settlements for the English.[7]

Throughout his reign, King Henry VII was interested in securing commercial and discovery missions for his subjects. In the beginning of his administration, he established important laws. Bacon, who worked under him, recorded important information on his devotion to the improvement of his kingdom. With respect to trade, King Henry VII nullified ancient rights, privileges, and customs accorded to the German merchants by his predecessors and the parliament.[8] He created conditions that led to the increase of English merchants' foreign trade. Additionally, he reviewed the privileges formally granted to domestic corporations. In the nineteenth year of his reign, King Henry VII took a different path toward the privileges granted to the masters and wardens of fellowships or corporations. He restricted corporate masters and wardens from making new bylaws.[9] Similarly, they were stopped from pricing wares and other goods according to their own wills. To remedy this abuse, King Henry VII entrusted the lords with the power to examine and approve the price of wares and other merchandise owned by the corporations. It is sound to stipulate that King Henry VII was against the exploitation of his subjects by commercial entities.

Regarding foreign trade, King Henry VII took a different approach compared to his predecessors. He signed various trade treaties with many kingdoms such as Denmark, France, Spain, Netherlands, Rome, and Ireland. The treaties were concluded for the interests of his countrymen. Moreover, the protections of his sailors were also noted in the treaties, as was the safeguarding of foreign traders on English soil and those traveling along English waterways. To illustrate this, in 1490, he signed an important treaty between England and Denmark.[10] In this treaty, King Henry VII negotiated good trade terms and conditions for his merchants, especially those of Bristol. This trade was enjoyed by merchants who commercialized with Iceland. English merchants sold material rough in texture, cloths, and other commodities to that area. These same privileges were also accorded to the citizens of Denmark. Pertaining the treaty with Denmark, Henry Duff Trail says that "this was an exclusive privilege, and was, no doubt well worth obtaining."[11]

In 1506, King Henry VII signed a commercial treaty with King Philip of the Netherlands.[12] In the same year, he also concluded a trade treaty with Castile, one which privileged English merchants with the same terms and conditions as that of Denmark.[13] As he did with the Netherlands, King Henry VII secured a treaty with France that abolished all imposts or tolls charged to merchants of both countries for forty-seven years preceding that treaty.[14] This agreement was critical for the maintenance and development of their free market, allowing merchants on all sides to increase their profits. During the reigns of King Henry VII and his predecessors, the majority of England's foreign trade was conducted by water highways. Thus, it was critical for England to have a navy powerful enough to deter her enemies.

During the period under examination, the navy was an important tool used for the transportation of military men and the protection of commerce. Upon the ascension of King Henry VII to the throne, England did not have an institutionalized navy and was poorly equipped militarily.

To remedy this, King Henry VII built a powerful navy, which had never existed before in the kingdom. According to English historians such as Adam Anderson, David Hume, and others, King Henry VII was the first monarch to establish a royal navy. He was also the first king to appoint an admiral, a position that was first held by Sir Edward Howard. With such a powerful navy, English sailors and merchants felt protected.

During the reign of King Henry VII, Pope Alexander VI divided the southern part of America between the Spanish and Portuguese kings.[15] These two kings were recognized as the owners of South America and West Africa through the rights of discovery. The king of Portugal claimed Africa as his land because Portuguese sailors were the first white people to reach it during the discovery era. On the other hand, the king of Spain claimed South America as his territory due to the discovery mission conducted by Christopher Columbus. However, regardless of what Pope Alexander declared, Adam Anderson writes that King Henry VII did not pay attention to any of those divisions.[16]

Likewise, the exploitation of discovery missions of the unknown lands continued without interruption after the death of Henry VII's father. The first communication relating to the service of Sebastian on behalf of the government of King Henry VIII was initiated by Robert Thorne, an English merchant who resided in Seville.[17] In that capacity, he was deeply interested in the discovery of new lands for the English. According to Francesco Tarducci, Thorne desired his country to fully engage in the discovery missions. Like Thorne, Cardinal Thomas Wolsey, Henry VIII's prime minister, made a substantive offer to Sebastian Cabot if he would serve the kingdom of England and explore new lands.[18] Cardinal Wolsey was the son of a butcher who resided in Ipswich, England. This butcher educated his son to the level that he became employed by powerful politicians in England.[19] He was an official distributor of alms to past kings, as well as King Henry VIII. David Hume, an English historian, notes that Cardinal Wolsey was the tutor of the children of the Marquess of Dorset. As a member of that family, his entrance to the royal court was not a matter of concern. As such, he was recommended by the marquess to be employed as chaplain to Henry VII. He was also entrusted with secret negotiation pertaining the king's marriage with Margaret of Savoy, Maximilian's daughter.[20]

There is evidence indicating that in 1511, when King Henry VIII entered the league of Spain against the king of France, Lord Willoughby, one of his generals in the expedition, took with him Sebastian Cabot as a tactician of war. Understanding that the kingdom's navy was poorly equipped and needed an upgrade, King Henry VIII ordered the building of the Royal Navy.[21] With such a powerful navy, the discovery missions of his subjects were increased. The historical records indicate that various English explored the unknown land during his reign. Like his father, King Henry VIII also supported the voyages of Sebastian Cabot. During his reign, Cabot communicated with Sir Thomas Spert, the vice admiral of England, regarding a voyage to Brazil. Accordingly, Sir Spert procured him a ship in the name of King Henry VIII.[22] Henry Richard Fox Bourne believes that in 1517, King Henry VIII furnished some ships for the expedition of Sebastian Cabot and Sir Thomas Spert.[23] The support from King Henry VIII to Cabot indicates that he followed the same maritime and discovery missions as King Henry VII. It is clear that the kingdom of England was engaged deeply in discovery missions. The discovery of new territories in America became a settled policy that the crowns of England had to accomplish. In the same context of discovery, William Hawkins voyaged to South America and has been credited as the founder of the English commerce with South America.[24] It seems that he was the first English man to travel to that part of the New World. Like him, his adopted son, John Hawkins, was also in the service of King Henry VIII from 1513 to 1518.[25]

King Henry VIII was likely open to the discovery missions of his subjects. In 1879, James Hannay, author of the *History of Acadia, from Its Discovery to the Surrender to England, by the Treaty of Paris*, writes that Thomas Thorne, a learned and wealthy resident of Bristol, wrote a letter to the king requesting his support for discovery missions. In 1512, King Henry VIII appointed Sir Edward Howard the First Lord Admiral. Similarly, a royal office for the admiral was established.[26]

As they had been during the reign of King Henry VIII, discovery missions in England were also undertaken during the administration of King Edward. Historians devoted to investigations of the discovery of the New World indicate that King Edward VI was interested in the maritime explorations of his subjects. To illustrate, during this reign, Sebastian Cabot was made the grant pilot of England. Furthermore, the Company of Merchant Adventurers, established by his subjects, was incorporated. This company centered its efforts on trade and discovery missions. The Branch of Bristol merchants was incorporated on December 23, 1552.[27] In regard to the service of Cabot, King Edward gave him a present of £200 as a matter of encouragement.[28] It appears that King Edward VI and the British citizens were delighted with the work Cabot accomplished for the honor of their kingdom. On May 9, 1553, during the reign of King Edward VI, Cabot was elected governor of the Mysterie and Companie of the Merchants Adventurers for the discovery of regions, dominions, islands, and unknown places.[29] With respect to the commercial company organized by merchant adventurers, Patrick Colquhoun writes that, after the charter was obtained from King Edward, members of the company set the capital for that enterprise at £6,000. Each effective member was required to pay twenty-five pounds.[30]

In 1558, with the ascension of Queen Elizabeth to the throne of England, the military and navy policies of the kingdom helped it emerge to a superpower level. Queen Elizabeth modernized the navy and military institutions. According to William Camden, this wise queen increased the salary of soldiers and the number of men stationed at the garrison. Camden also notes that the Garrison of Barwick, which had five hundred men, saw its numbers increase during the reign of Queen Elizabeth. It is important to stipulate that the increase of military men at the garrison signified a deterrence posture to the country's enemies. In addition to the improvements of the garrisons, Queen Elizabeth freed the kingdom from armament dependency. Camden writes that "she was the first that procured gun powder to be made in England that she might not both pray and pay for it also to her neighbors."[31] Queen Elizabeth permitted the use of her navy equipment by her subjects. This navy was ready to attack the enemies of the kingdom of England. In the same period, the numbers of sailors and marines were increased by the request of Queen Elizabeth. In like manner, she increased the number of ships for trade for the regions of Hamborough, Lubeck, Dantzick, Genoa, and Venice.[32] Following the example of their queen, English seamen and merchants were seduced into purchasing warships for trade as well as for discovery missions.[33]

Relating to discovery missions, historical data reveals that, during the reign of Queen Elizabeth, George Barnes, William Gerard, and Anthony Hudsey, under the command of Sir Hugh Willoughby, traveled to Cathay. Along their way, Sir Willoughby froze to death. On the other hand, Richard Chancellor, who was in a different vessel, made his way to Russia. Camden notes that he discovered a passage to Russia.[34] This discovery seems to be the first of that kind organized during the reign of Queen Elizabeth. In addition to the English explorers mentioned previously, during Queen Elizabeth's reign, Sir John Hawkins, Francis Drake, John Oxenham, and Sir Humphrey Gilbert were engaged in discovery missions. These English seamen explored various places in the world unknown to their countrymen. For example, Sir John Hawkins traveled to Africa and the Bay of Mexico.[35] During his voyages in Africa, Sir John Hawkins captured Africans and sold them into slavery in the Americas. During this same period, he sold them to Brazil or other Spanish islands such as Hispaniola. In addition to the seamen named previously, Martin Frobisher was also an adamant seaman devoted to the discovery missions. William Robertson writes that, when the Earl of Warwick planned his discovery scheme, he employed Martin Frobisher to accomplish the same. Robertson also posited that Frobisher was an experienced seaman with a great reputation in that field.[36]

In 1578, Queen Elizabeth granted a patent to Sir Humphrey Gilbert of Devon County, England, to find land not occupied by Christian princes or people so that he could settle or occupy it. In 1584, Queen Elizabeth also granted a letter patent to Adrian Gilbert for the same purpose. In the same year, Sir Walter Raleigh received a patent from Queen Elizabeth. Furthermore, in addition to issuing patents, the English crowns established productive economic policies for their countrymen. Data from the *State Papers* indicate that Sir Raleigh was encouraged by Queen Elizabeth in his mission of planting the first English colony in America.[37]

After Queen Elizabeth died, King James I was coronated. With respect to the discovery and exploration missions, this king has been characterized by English scholars as being a selfish monarch. Instead of focusing on overseas discoveries, he paid much more attention to the establishment of plantations in Ireland and Scotland for his security design. In addition to the negligence of productive policy on the colonization movement, he has also been accused of focusing on the patronage system. He privileged his family friends, government members, and wealthy men with obtaining the land discovered in North America. In relation to the colonization movement, data indicate that he issued many charter patents to various government officials, as well as family friends. Among those who accused King James I as helpless in the domain of colonization was Lucy Aikin. In her *Memoirs of the Court of King Charles the First, Vol. 1*, Aikin says that King James I contributed nothing but his credentials or letter patents.[38] Aikin goes on to stipulate that, during his reign, English merchants complained consistently but in vain. They requested his protection, but the king did not afford it to them.[39] To support her account of the negligence of King James I toward English merchants and seamen, she gave tangible examples of such abuse, which was witnessed by Thomas Roe, an English ambassador to Constantinople. According to Aikin, at the port of Messina, the English captured by the Spanish were imprisoned in the galley of the Turk in miserable conditions. They were captured by the Spanish and sold to the Turks, and they were pressed into their service.[40] In the same context of the issuing of letter patents, William Robertson posits that

"King James I, who prided himself on his profound skill in the science of government, and who had turned his attention to consider the advantages which might be derived from colonies, at a time when he patronized his scheme for planting them in some of the ruder provinces of his ancient kingdom, with a view of introducing industry and civilization there, was now no less fond of directing the active genius of his English subjects towards occupations not repugnant to his own maxims, and listened with a [favorable] ear to their application."[41]

The complaints of these writers are sound because, during King James I's reign, many English people were abused in Newfoundland. In 1618, Dover's merchants were angered by the French attacks upon them in Newfoundland. On October 19, 1628, the Earl of Bath sent a petition from the merchants of Devon to the Privy Council, requesting some security measures for their fishing industry in Newfoundland.[42] This incident happened during the reign of King James I. On March 16, 1620, John Mason, the governor of Newfoundland, did the same. He pleaded to the King James I to annually assign a lieutenant in Newfoundland, with a mandate to guard the coasts against pirates. Moreover, Governor Mason noted that the duties of the lieutenant also included dealing with the preservation of good order for the fishing fleet.[43] It seems that King James I did not take any measure to satisfy the same.

Even though King James I has been accused of being a despot, in his first Parliament convened in November 1605, he was devoted to the development of his kingdom and his countrymen. Under his power, the English aim of discovering new territory for the kingdom increased. During this period, the colonization movement was taken into consideration by the English, hoping to increase power and wealth for the kingdom. For that reason, many people of ranks and noblemen were interested in the colonization scheme. Among the influential people who supported such movement were Robert Cecil, Earl of Salisbury; Sir John Popham, Lord Chief Justice; Henry Wriothesley, Third Earl of Southampton; and Sir Ferdinando Gorges. On April 10, 1606, King James I granted to Sir Thomas Gates; Sir George Somers; Richard Hakluyt, prebendary of Westminster; Edward Maria Wingfield; Thomas Hamon; Raleigh Gilbert; William Parker; George Popham; and diverse others the territories of Virginia situated between 34 and 45 degrees north latitude, which was to be divided into two colonies.[44] This was the first time those regions were called Southern Virginia and Northern Virginia. The first section of the territory was given to the London Company, and the second to the Plymouth Company.[45] To satisfy his aim, King James I formed a council with the power of supervision of the colonies.[46] It was under his reign that Virginia, the first English colony in North America, was planted by Sir Walter Raleigh. On March 3, 1620, the Council for New England and associates from western England petitioned to the king with the vision of establishing a plantation in Northern Virginia. In the petition, they requested for King James I to offer them the same privileges as he gave to the Virginia colony. In addition, they wanted an enlargement of their territory, which was to be called New England. In the same year, the Council of Plymouth was incorporated.

On November 3, 1620, the Council for New England Colony was incorporated by King James. After the incorporation of this association, the Duke of Lennox, the Marquis of Buckingham, and others were entrusted with the power to govern the New England colony, which was situated between 40 and 48 degrees north latitude. The power given to members of the Council of New England included the selection of forty members for that entity.[47]

After the death of King James I, Charles was coronated. Evidence indicates that during his reign, King Charles I continued with the same policy as his predecessor, issuing letter patents to noblemen and wealthy people who desired to establish colonies in North America, especially in Northern Virginia, which was what the English explorers called the New England region during that era. The major outcome of colonization under Charles I's reign was the incorporation of the Governor and the Company of Massachusetts Bay in New England in 1629. This incorporated company was assigned to Sir Henry Roswell, Sir John Young, Thomas Southcote, John Humphrey, John Endecott, and Simon Whitcombe, their heirs, and associates which was the beginning of the Massachusetts Bay Colony.[48] It is sound to note that the English listed previously were the first architects of the planting of Massachusetts Bay in New England.

Chapter 2

The Plymouth Company
and the Council for New England

The colonization of New England can be traced from the discovery missions of the Plymouth and Bristol seamen. Merchants and prominent men in Devonshire also devoted their time and energy to the discovery missions. In the previous chapter, the exploration missions undertaken by the Plymouth and Bristol seamen were passionately stated. However, the structure and the vision of their discovery took a different magnitude after the voyages of Captain Bartholomew Gosnold and Sir John Smith.

From the time of Sir Francis Drake's explorations of New England, the English did not establish settlements or plantations in that region. Contrary to the exploration of Sir Drake, in 1602, Captain Gosnold traveled to a portion of New England land that was later called Massachusetts Bay. According to William Robertson, Captain Gosnold named the discovered region Cape Cod.[1] John Josselyn, the Scottish traveler, says that Captain Gosnold extended the exploration of New England territories.[2] Like Josselyn, George Bancroft notes that Captain Gosnold made an expedition to New England, which was supported by the Earl of Southampton. Bancroft wrote with authority that Captain Gosnold established the first English colony in Cape Elizabeth, on the coast of Maine.[3] The account of Bancroft about the establishment of a permanent English colony by Gosnold is disputable. Even though Bancroft notes a permanent colony in Maine, data from historical documents do not support the existence of a permanent colony in New England before the arrival of the Pilgrims in New Plymouth. It is acceptable to speculate that Bancroft was referring to the first permanent fort for the English.

As we noted in the beginning, Captain Smith's expedition to New England in 1614 brought new information relating to that region. Upon his return to England, he made a map that described the New England territory better than former maps, rousing the interest of merchants and colonization promoters. Before his trip, some attempts were made to plant colonies in New England, but none were successful. To illustrate this, in 1604, French Huguenot Du Mont, with Champlain and other people of the same religion, attempted to establish a colony at the mouth of Saint Croix, but they failed. In 1606, in England, Sir John Popham was interested in forming a colony in the northern parts of America. Consequently, he encouraged citizens of Plymouth to do the same. On May 20, 1606, Walter Matthew, the mayor, and members of the city council of Plymouth communicated with Sir Robert Cecil on that subject. Alexander Brown documented that Sir Robert Cecil was a partner of the southern colony. Lord Justice Sir John Popham was the patron of the northern colony.[4] The result of the colonization communication between the Plymouth people and Sir Robert Cecil could not be found at the time of the writing of this book. But during the second year of the First Parliament of King James I, the prospect of colonizing New England was discussed.

The Plymouth Company

The Plymouth Company was more than likely established in 1606, even though it remained unincorporated. As noted in the previous paragraph, King James I and his Parliament were motivated by the interest that the English had in the colonization movement. As a result, on June 6, 1606, an act was passed to satisfy the same. Alexander Brown writes that "it was during this period of excitement, and under the same influence, that the national movement for securing a land or plantation in the New World for the English race and religion, was taken definite shape in England."[5] During this parliamentary session, members decided to entrust such missions to a certain group of people. Accordingly, Sir Robert Cecil, the Earl of Salisbury; Lord Chief Justice Sir John Popham; Henry Wriothesley, the Third Earl of Southampton; and Sir Ferdinando Gorges were empowered with the colonization scheme of the New World. The document that entrusted these individuals with the architecture of the colonization movement was signed by Sir Thomas Gates.[6] The account of Brown regarding the involvement of Sir John Popham and Sir Ferdinando Gorges is undisputable. In 1887, William Hunt recorded that members of the Plymouth Company, such as Chief Justice Popham and Sir Ferdinando Gorges, were ardent promoters. According to Hunt, Sir Popham planted a colony upon the Sagadahoc River, but the colony was abandoned.[7] In addition to the two promoters listed previously, the Devonshire Association for the Advancement of Science, Literature, and Arts added Thomas Hanham, Raleigh Gilbert, William Parker, and George Popham as some of the earliest promoters of the colonization movements. This association also pointed out that advertisements were made in Plymouth, Bristol, and Exeter for this company.[8] The advertisements were conducted to motivate new members to join the company. Merchants in western England were not as wealthy as those from London. Therefore, the Plymouth Company needed reliable and moneyed associates who would contribute to the advancement of the colonization missions. In addition to the cities named previously, London merchants were also invited to join the Plymouth Company. In this case, we find James Mason as a member of the Plymouth Company. With the formation of this company, its agents attempted several times to establish colonies in New England.

Colonization Attempts by the Plymouth Company

The history pertaining to colonization attempts made by the Plymouth Company's members has been written by various historians: John Josselyn, William Hubbard, and others. From 1606 until the establishment of the New Plymouth Colony, many attempts were made to establish colonies in New England. For example, John Josselyn notes that in 1607, Plymouth Plantation was founded. Sir John Popham, Lord Chief of Justice and speaker of the House of Commons was the principal financial backer. His nephew George Popham, who led the group built a fort at the mouth of Sagadahoc River. This fort was established when George Popham was the president at Sagadahoc River.[9] In 1622, Thomas Weston, a member of the Plymouth Company, attempted to establish a plantation in Massachusetts and named the place Weymouth.[10]

The Incorporation of the Plymouth Company

On March 3, 1620, New Plymouth Company members petitioned King James to incorporate their business entity. In this petition, they asked the king to empower them with the same privileges as the London Company. They also requested that the territory under their company be called New England. On November 3, 1620, the Council for New England was incorporated by King James during the fourth year of his reign. This organization was formed of most noted people in western England, precisely, the merchants of Bristol, Exeter, and Plymouth. According to historians, this organization was at first called the Plymouth Company. According to *Calendar of the State Papers, Colonial Series*, the patent of incorporation of the Plymouth Company was issued to the Duke of Lennox, the Marquis of Buckingham, and to other members of the council that was established in Plymouth. They had the power of establishing and governing plantations. In like manner, they were also permitted to choose forty people as its members. On that same date, the Marquis of Buckingham was officially recognized as president of the Council for the Plantation of New England.[11]

Wealthy men, government officials, and adventurers from the western part of England composed this group. Among the powerful people who were part of this council, others included: Lodwick, Duke of Lennox; Lord Stewart, Lord Marquis Hamilton, high admiral of England; James, Marquis Hamilton; William, Earl of Pembroke; Thomas, Earl of Arundel; William, Earl of Bath; Henry, Earl of Southampton; William, Earl of Salisbury; Robert, Earl of Warwick; John, Viscount of Haddington; Edward, Lord of Zouch; Edmund, Lord Sheffield; Edward, Lord Gorges; Sir Edward Seynor, Sir Robert Mansel, Sir Nathaniel Rich, Robert Heath, and Raleigh Gilbert.

This council formed a body politic for the planting, ruling, ordering, and governing of New England in America. As such, the council had the power to issue land patents to those who desired planting settlements or colonies in the New England region. Regarding patentees, records indicate that Reverend White of Dorchester purchased a patent from the Council of New England for the establishment of a fishery company at Cape Anne in 1624. His patent was the first issued for that purpose in western New England. The scheme of the Dorchester Company in Massachusetts was a failure.

On March 19, the Council of New England sold their jurisdiction to the Massachusetts Bay Company.[12] With the creation of the Massachusetts Bay Company, Sir Henry Roswell, Sir John Humphrey, John Endecott, and Simon Whitcombe, their heirs, and associates became the sole owners of the Massachusetts Bay Company.[13] On March 4, 1629, the Massachusetts Bay Company was chartered by the king, and it became a corporation under the name of Governor and Company of the Massachusetts Bay in New England.[14] This charter of a part of New England was granted to John Endecott, Theophilus Eaton, and others.[15]

Chapter 3

A Demographic History of the Founders of the New England Colonies

The study of regulatory laws in the New England colonies must not be examined without reference to the demographic history of its founders. The qualities, designs, and visions of the leaders who settled in New England are important in order to understand the laws and regulations they enacted. Likewise, the initial designs of the supporters of the colonization movement must be understood in the context of how the plan for the colonization of New England was envisioned by influential people in England. To illustrate, Sir Robert Naunton favored the immigration of Puritans to the New World. He discussed this design with the king.[1] Like Sir Naunton, the Earl of Lincoln was also a supporter of the Puritans.[2] In fact, two of his daughters were part of the group who immigrated to New England. Lady Arbella and her sister, Susan Arbella, both the daughters of the Earl of Lincoln, travelled to New England. Lady Arbella was the wife of Isaac Johnson, and Susan was the wife of John Humphrey. Susan's husband traveled to New England in 1634, even though he was chosen as deputy governor of the Massachusetts Bay Company.[3] Furthermore, Sir Edwin Sandy was also a sympathizer of the Pilgrims. At the time when he was treasurer of the Virginia Company, he was involved in the negotiations regarding the immigration of Pilgrims to Virginia. Moreover, Theophilus Clinton, the fourth Earl of Lincoln, was close to Cotton Mather in Boston, England. Another person who was interested in the colonization movement was Sir Robert Gorges.

In 1623, the Council for New England sent an officer with the power to protect land under their jurisdiction against trespassing fishermen. However, the officer dispatched by the Council for New England was incapable of deterring the fishermen.[4] According to the *Records of the Colony of the Massachusetts Bay in New England* from 1619, there was an increase in fishermen activities in the New England region. These fishermen were from the western part of Great Britain, and they were not licensed to fish in that region.[5] In 1624, Robert Cushman was also involved in the colonization movement of the Pilgrims.[6] He was their chief representative, and one of his duties was to purchase a patent from the Council of New England for the planting of a settlement in Cape Anne. With his efforts, they received a patent, which was issued by Lord Sheffield.[7] During this negotiation, he was assisted by Edward Winslow.

Before the establishment of the Massachusetts Bay Colony, various colonization attempters settled in New England without success. For example, Thomas Weston, a merchant from London, established a plantation in Massachusetts, but it did not last for long. Likely, Robert Gorges, son of Sir Ferdinando Gorges, did the same.[8] Robert Gorges was commissioned by the Council of New England as governor-general to the entire land covering the village of Weymouth, formerly Wessagusset.[9] On his way to New England, Gorges was accompanied by William Morell, an Episcopalian clergyman, who was entrusted with the enforcement of religious affairs.[10]

In addition to the listed leaders, many influential men in England were also interested in the colonization of New England. Viscounts Saye and Sele and Lord Brooke obtained a patent to establish a settlement at the Connecticut River. They were helped by the Earl of Warwick, the president of the New England Council in 1631. Viscount Saye and Sele and Lord Brooke were also included on the same patent as the Earl of Warwick. In addition to the two officials named previously, their closest friends and relatives were also part of the patent assigned to the Earl of Warwick. The accounts regarding the inclusions of English dignitaries in the colonization scheme gives us ample understanding about the reason why the New England colonies were better organized than their brethren in Virginia. These listed officials were deeply involved in the colonization missions in North America, especially in the New England colonies.

Historically, the founders of the New England colonies emigrated from various parts of England. As an illustration of this, the first English who established a settlement in Cape Anne were from Dorchester, England. Historians from Massachusetts, such as Joseph Barlow Felt, agree that the settlement of Salem was first intended as a fishing enterprise from Dorchester, and was originally orchestrated by Rev. John White of the county, who strongly supported the establishment of a colony in Massachusetts and sent Dorchester men to accomplish this goal.[11] As a result, he sent Dorchester men to accomplish this goal. White received a great deal of praise from various writers with respect to his contributions to the New England colonization scheme. According to the Dorchester Antiquarian and Historical Society, Rev. White was the rector of Trinity Parish in Dorsetshire, England. In 1623, he was engaged in the New England fishery with Dorchester adventurers. This association gathered £3,000 sterling with the objective of planting a settlement on the shores of New England. In addition to this business enterprise, the intended settlement was also reserved as an asylum community for English citizens who had been prosecuted based on their religious and political beliefs.[12]

Historically, King James I had assigned the New England regions to western England merchants and noblemen at the time when he divided the territory of Virginia into two parts, Southern and Northern Virginia. From the grants of King James of 1606, the New England region was placed under the jurisdiction of merchants from Plymouth, Bristol, Exeter, and from other parts of western England. The granting of the New England region to the merchants of Plymouth, Bristol, and Exeter was historic. From the beginning of the discovery movement, men from western England labored intensively, searching for new lands in that region. As an example, seamen and merchants who traveled with John and Sebastian Cabot were from western England, especially Bristol. Much of the aggressive exploration of the New England territories was done by sailors from western England. Sir John Hawkins, an adopted son of Plymouth, is one notable example, as is Sir Francis Drake; both were inhabitants of Bristol. Even the Southern Virginia region was established due to the steadfastness of a Bristol merchant.[13] William Paterson, the author of *The Merchant Princes of England*, elucidates that data from the petition of Walter Barrett, Walter Sandy, and a company of Bristol merchants indicated that the listed people and merchants had been establishing plantations in New England many years before the mass movement to that region.[14]

Information recorded by William Paterson covering the western England inhabitants in New England is supported by Abiel Holmes. He writes that many immigrants in Massachusetts were from western England, but there was a large number from the vicinity of London. Two examples of this were Sir Richard Saltonstall and John Mason, both of whom were wealthy men from London. In addition to the previously named Massachusetts Bay officials, Matthew Cradock, the first governor of the Massachusetts Bay Company, was from London.[15]

Connecticut historians, as well as the Dorchester Historical Society in Massachusetts, believe that the early settlers in Dorchester were from Devon, Dorset, and Somerset. Data from the *Report of the Devonshire Association for the Advancement of Science, Literature and Arts* indicate that New England settlements were inhabited by people from the western counties in England, particularly Devon, Cornwall, Somerset, and Dorset.[16] Accordingly, English settlers who came from those counties were associated with Rev. John White, the father of the Massachusetts immigration movement. Henry Stiles, author of *The History of Ancient Windsor, Connecticut*, called Rev. White the "great patron of New England emigration."[17] Historically, Rev. White was an indefatigable visionary in his work on the colonization scheme. After the failure of his Dorchester Company, he engaged with the Massachusetts Bay Company for the same purpose. It appears that the colonization movement was one of his missions for his country and his people. Another Massachusetts Bay Company official of note from Dorchester was John Endecott. According to John Brown, Governor Endecott was a native of Dorchester and a faithful Puritan. While in Dorchester, he attended the teaching of Samuel Skelton, a minister who traveled to New England in 1629.[18]

In the same context of western England, in 1623, King James I wrote a letter to the Lord Lieutenants of Cornwall, Somerset, and Devon, as well as to the cities of Bristol and Exeter, to look for quality people to join the colonization movement in New England.[19] The king stressed that the planting of New England was a work of great interest to the public. He went on to declare that "the subsequent grant was for a general and free Constitution for the maintenance of the plantation."[20]

In addition to western England, some historians believe that eastern England was also involved in the colonization schemes. Data regarding men from eastern England have been noted by many writers such as Joseph Hopkins Twichell, Robert Charles Winthrop, Ezra S. Stearns, Samuel Abbott Green, William Bradford, and William B. Weeden. In his book *Economic and Social History of New England, 1620–1789*, Weeden noted that the New England colonies were inhabited by a large population of immigrants from the eastern parts of England. He went on, stipulating that English from the eastern part of the country were of German and Scandinavian ancestry.[21] His account is undisputable because data from various documents lists names of settlers in these regions from eastern England. Moreover, John Camden Hotten, the author of *The Original Lists of Persons* agrees with the perception of Weeden. In this work, Hotten mentioned the immigration of men from Essex County in England.[22] According to him, men from Essex County went to New England in 1637 and 1638. He noted that Governor John Haynes was an Essex man.[23] Frederic Calvin Norton documented that his parents were from Codicote in Hertford County. According to Norton's account, the Haynes family was wealthy and long-standing in Hertford County. Due to their wealth, they owned valuable properties such as land in Hertford and Essex. In the colony, he was elected governor in Massachusetts and in Connecticut.[24]

John Brown, who wrote about the Pilgrims in 1895, articulates also that men from Lincolnshire were associated with the colonization of New England. His account was based on the contributions made by the Gainsborough Pilgrims and that of John Winthrop. According to his collections, one-sixth of New England inhabitants were from Devon, Dorset, and Somerset. On the other hand, he stated that the remaining inhabitants were from other parts of England, including the counties of Lincoln, Norfolk, Suffolk, and Essex.[25] According to him, the design of the Plymouth Colony began at Gainsborough, which was a town in Lincolnshire, and was also a Puritan fiefdom like Scrooby. Brown went on to stipulate that when John Winthrop was appointed governor, many Suffolk Puritans migrated to America.[26] Just like Winthrop was from Groton Manor in Lincolnshire, his countrymen followed him to New England. The accounts of these writers are unquestionable. Many important officials in the New England colonies were from the eastern part of England. Simon Bradstreet, Isaac Johnson, William

Coddington, John Endecott, Thomas Dudley, Richard Bellingham, and Thomas Leverett were from Boston, Lincolnshire, in England. Among these people, a few of them were elected governors in Massachusetts Bay and Rhode Island. Thomas Dudley, Bellingham, Leverett, and Bradstreet were governors in Massachusetts Bay. On the other hand, William Coddington was governor in Rhode Island in Newport.

Another person of note from Lincolnshire was Simon Bradstreet. In England, he was associated with Earl of Lincoln. He attended Cambridge for one year before being appointed steward to the countess of Warwick.[27] Like those from Boston in Lincolnshire, in the county of Suffolk, in the southern part of the Eastern Suffolk County, John Winthrop and his son of the same name were elected governors. The father was governor of Massachusetts Bay for many years with some interruption. On the other hand, John Winthrop, Jr. was the governor of Connecticut. Many of these officials will be discussed later in this chapter, when we tackle their qualities.

Previously in this chapter, we noted that New England inhabitants were descendants of Anglo-Saxons and Scandinavians, as noted by Weeden. Like Weeden, various American historians have employed the term *Anglo-Saxon* while identifying the colonists in the American colonies. To illustrate, Brooks, author of the *History of the Town of Medford, Middlesex County*, noted that on June 17, 1630, their Anglo-Saxon ancestors arrived at Medford, and they made it a settlement for the town.[28]

Due to these illustrations, I was driven to give a brief history of the entrance of Germanic tribes in Britain. From various documents consulted, data recorded by English historians show that eastern England was conquered by the Saxon and Angles, both Germanic tribes; the western and southern parts of Britain faced the same fate. English authors such as John Stow, Sharon Turner, Thomas Wright, and Saint Bede the Venerable noted that, due to attacks from the Picts and Scots, the Britons consulted among themselves, and their councils authorized their King Vortigern to invite the Saxons as guest militiamen.[29] According to Bede, the Saxons, Angles, and Jutes were Germanic tribes who assisted the Britons' military against the Pics and Scots.[30] The account of Bede does not stipulate whether the term *Saxons* represented a single tribe or a union of tribes.

Contrary to Bede, Wilhelm Zimmermann described the German tribes with authority. He notes that the Saxons were a collection of many tribes, which he termed the league of Saxons. According to him, in the history of Germany, the Saxons were agglomerated as a confederation around the third century.[31] He also articulated that the different Saxon tribes were related by blood and speech. In his book *A Popular History of Germany: From the Earliest to the Present Day*, he reveals that the Chauci, Angarii, Cherusci, and Western Frisians were part of the Saxon confederation. This group of people resided in Holstein, Schleswig, and Jutland.[32] Like Zimmermann, Bayard Taylor asserts that the confederate of Saxon tribes had the same characteristics.[33] In the same view as to the arrival of the Germanic tribes in England, many English writers, such as John Whitaker, believe that Hengist and Horsa, the leaders of the German tribes, descended from the Jutes tribe.[34]

According to Zimmermann, Hengist and Horsa entered Briton through the River Thanet.[35] From the work of John Whitaker, we discovered that Hengist and Horsa were Jutes. According to him, this tribe landed in Briton around 447 equipped with three ships.[36] The entrance port of the Jutes in Briton was described by Julius Caesar as Cantium, which was located at the mouth of the Thames River. Before the arrival of the Romans, Cantium, or Kent, was governed by four kings, namely, Cingetorix, Carvilius, Taximagulus, and Segovax.[37] This region was inhabited by the Cantii. Before the arrival of the Romans, the island of Briton was inhabited by many tribes. British scholars and historians have recorded pertinent facts on the tribes that inhabited the island. The Brigantes, Iceni, Trinobantes, Cantii, Belgae, the Bibroci, Cassi, Ancalites, and the Segontioci were Briton tribes as recorded by Thomas Wright.[38] In regard to the invitation of German tribes to Briton, George William Spencer presented the same data with minor differences. He stipulated that due to the attacks of the Pics and Scots, Vortigern, the King of Devonshire and Cornwall, proposed the invitation of Saxon troops for the protection of Britain. His proposal was received with enthusiasm.[39] As a result, ambassadors were sent to the Saxons' land for military aid. Upon their arrival among the Germanic tribes, they had a meeting with Witigisil, the commander in chief of the Saxons. Witigisil called an assembly of his people. At the general meeting of the Saxons under Witigisil, it was decided that militiamen should be sent to Britain under the command of Witigisil's two sons, Hengist and Horsa.[40]

This account pertaining to the arrival of the Saxon tribes under the command of Hengist and Horsa has been challenged by a segment of British scholars such as Sir Francis Palgrave, Henry Charles Coote, and John Beddoe. According to the analysis of Henry Charles Coote, Hengist and Horsa, who Saint Bede recorded as the leader of the Saxons during the invasion of Briton, did not exist. From his own research, he discovered the name of Wyrtgeorn as the old leader of the Jutes in Britain.[41] Even though Coote discovered that Wyrtgeon was the leader of the Jutes in Britain, he failed to answer how he arrived on that island. Was he born in Britain? Were the Jutes a tribe among the Britons? These questions are salient to the study of the arrival of Germanic tribes in Britain. In this case, if Wyrtgeorn was a leader of the Jutes in Britain after the departure of the Romans, it is worth asserting that Germanic tribes were in Britain before their full invasion of that island.

Historically, Sir Palgrave, Thomas Wright, and Henry Charles Coote note the existence of Germanic tribes in Britain before and during the administrations of the Romans. In his work titled *The Romans of Britain*, Coote says that Italian writers mentioned that Romans recruited Germanic tribes into the ranks of their army. He noted that mercenary soldiers entered into an alliance with the Romans, but such service was often disrupted.[42] Coote's assertions about the inclusion of Germans in the ranks of the Roman Army is supported by the work of Cornelius Tacitus. Tacitus's work is authoritative in design; he received his information from his father-in-law, Agricola. Agricola did recruit Germanic tribes during his invasion of Britain. According to Tacitus, Agricola's army was formed of Romans and men raised in Germany. He lists them as Usipians, Batavians, and Tungrians. According to his work, the Usipii resided on the Rhine River, along with the Tencteri.[43]

Similar corroboration on the recruitment of Germanic tribes in the Roman Army was supported by Sir Francis Palgrave. In his book *History of the Anglo-Saxons*, he articulated that the Quadi and Marcomanni received a reward from the Romans for the possession of lands in Britain. He also noted the existence of Tungarian soldiers brought to Britain by Agricola. In addition to the authors already listed, John Beddoe, in his book *The Races of Britain: A Contribution to the Anthropology of Western Europe*, elucidates that Marcus Aurelius had with him Marcomanni captives from Germany when he went to Britain. Similarly, Probus had Alemanni as captives. The Alemanni's king was named Crocius. Like the Alemanni, Valentinian brought with him to Britain the Bucinobantes, a small Alemannic tribe residing near Magence.[44] These illustrations confirm that Germanic tribes were already in Britain before the full invasion or occupation of that island. The accounts of these writers reveal the participation of Germanic tribes in Britain, but they fail to explain how many Germanic tribes were recruited by Agricola. Did Germans recruited for military services under the Romans return to Germany after their military duties? If they had children, were their descendants Britons or Germans? These questions can be helpful in the analysis of the continuous residency of Germans in Britain. In this case, we can suppose that there existed German Britons during the Roman administrations. Moreover, there is data indicating that Julius Caesar was the architect of recruiting Germans into his service, and that this was continued by his successors.[45] Furthermore, in Germany, there were the Aestii, and one of the tribes of that nation spoke a language that resembled the language of the Britons. Were the Aestii also in the league of the Britons? With respect to Aestii, Cornelius Tacitus noted that they lived on the right shore of the Suevic Sea. He went on to note that their habits and customs were the same as those of the Suevi.[46]

According to records, the Jutes came from Jutland. They resided in the same region as their brethren, the Angles. The area where they lived is also called the Cimbric Chersonesus.[47] The Angles occupied Holstein in the district called Anglen or Land of the English. Regarding the Angli or Angles, Cornelius Tacitus records that they were a Suevic clan. He believed this tribe occupied the larger part of Schleswig-Holstein and probably the northern district of Hanover.[48] The Angrivarii, another German tribe, inhabited the west of Weser and Westaphalia. The Aviones, another Suevic clan, were associated with their brethren the Reugigni, Angli, Varini, Endoses, Suardones, and Nuithones. They occupied Mecklenburg-Schwerin, Mecklenburg Strelitz, and Schleswig-Holstein bordering the Elbe in the east.[49] On the other hand, the Batavi, a tribe of the Chalti, occupied the Island of the Rhine. The Tungarians were also Germans. As to the location of Germany, Julius Caesar posited that "Germania, an ancient Germany was bounded by the German Ocean and the Baltic, the Vistula, the Danube, and the Rhine."[50] His description of Germany makes us able to comprehend how the Germans traveled to Britain. Accordingly, the German Ocean is the area that separates both nations.

Regarding German tribes, it is important to consult the work of Germany's writers. As such, the work of Wilhem Zimmermann was of interest to this project. Zimmermann gives us a new concept regarding the existence of Germanic tribes in England. According to him, Julius Caesar noted that the Belgae were of German descent. If this is true, it is important to note that Germans were in England before the arrival of Hengist and Horsa, both Jutland men. It seems that Caesar's account is considerable regarding the Germanic nature of the Belgae. Many English writers have stated that the Belgae in Britain were German descendants. Henry Charles Coote quoted the work of Agricola written by Tacitus regarding the Belgae. According to Coote, the "Belgae of Britain resembled Belgae of Gaul; and were Germans and spoke the same language as that great race."[51] This account of Coote is pertinent. The collaboration of Belgae and their Germans relatives was indicated by Wilhelm Zimmermann. According to him, when the Belgae had a military confrontation with the Romans, they did call upon the Germans in the right bank of the Rhine for military assistance.[52] Accordingly, the Belgae were always proud of being part of a Germanic tribe. Zimmermann notes that the Gauls and the Belgians boasted of having German blood in their veins.[53] This shows that the Gauls and the Belgians were related to Germans by blood. During this era, tribes always sought military assistance within their own clans. Like the Belgae, the Frisians were also of German blood. Like the tribes listed previously, the Norwegians, Swedes, and Danes are also Germans. Zimmermann tells us that the Saxons were a confederacy of many tribes. They lived in the lower bank of the lower Elbe. The Angarii, or Angrivarii, were also Germans. Zimmermann explains that in the third century, the Angarii formed a confederation with other Germanic tribes that was called Saxon. Zimmermann went on to stipulate that a Saxon confederation of various tribes was connected by blood and speech. He listed tribes such as the Chauci, Angarii, Cherusci, and the Western Frisians as members of the Saxon confederation. In the third century, the northwestern part of Germany near the Franks was called the Saxon Union.[54] During the Roman reign, Germany was divided into lower and upper provinces and was called Germanias.[55] Wolfgang Menzel writes that the Saxon was a confederation of tribes such as Chauci, Frisii, and the rest of the tribes located on the coasts of the Norther and the Baltic.[56]

In addition to the Saxons, Jutes, and Angli, the Danes—another Germanic tribe—invaded the kingdom of England. The invasions of England by the Danes have been recorded by various historians in England. J. G. Edgar, in his book *Danes, Saxons, and Normans; or Stories of Our Ancestors,* notes that the Danes settled gradually in Northumberland, East Anglia, and Mercia. He went on to write that they occupied the whole part of the River Thames. As early as 871, the Danes killed King Ethelred during their invasion. As a result, his son, Alfred, was crowned king after his father's death. Like his father, King Alfred was also attacked by the Danes, but they were not successful. In 994, Sweyn, King of Denmark, with the assistance of Olaf, King of Norway, joined forces to subdue the English. Fearing these attacks, English kings agreed to pay the Danegeld (a yearly tax) to King Sweyn.[57]

Similar information regarding the Danes in England was elucidated by J. J. A. Worsaae. In his account of the Danes and Norwegians in England, Scotland, and Ireland, he writes that the Danes were a terror to the English people for three centuries. During this period, many of them married English women and increased their numbers in that kingdom.[58] According to his illustration, the Cumberland region was inhabited by many Danes and Norwegians. He also asserted that the Danes were under the power of the Anglo-Saxons in the middle of the eleventh century. Danes were also included in the army or militia of the kingdom. Worsaae recorded pertinent data on the employment of Danes by English kings as militiamen. According to him, in 1011, the Danish Vikings freely enlisted in the ranks of the English military service for a salary. This practice of engaging the Danes in the service of England started with King Ethelred and was continued by his successors. In 925, King Athelstan employed many Danish militiamen for the suppression of his enemies. The Danes also occupied the kingdom of England during the reign of King Canute. With these occupations, the Danes became part of the English tribes. The tribes listed above are among the ancestors of the English who immigrated to New England.

The Academic and Religious Qualities of New England Leaders

The qualities and demeanor of leaders who founded the New England colonies have been noted by many writers. Earlier New England historians such as Thomas Hutchinson, James Savage, Alice Morse Earle, Joseph Barlow Felt, and William Hubbard have recorded authentic data on the founding leaders of the regions under investigation. From these writers, we have learned that the architects of the New England colonialization movements were people of high public standing and prominence in their native land. They matriculated in universities such as Cambridge and Oxford, and others likely attended divinity colleges.

The qualities of the New England leaders were clearly stated by Alice Morse Earle in her book, *Customs and Fashions in Old New England*. According to Earle, "the plantations in New England were inhabited by men of special intelligence, and almost universally of good education, it was inevitable that early and profound attention should be paid to the establishment of schools."[59] Her views regarding the scholarship of New England leaders were the same as those of Benjamin Peirce. In his *History of Harvard University*, Peirce writes that the first settlers of New England were educated in renowned institutions in England. He pointed out that they went to various universities in their mother countries and understood the value of education.[60] Among those who entered colleges was Rev. John Harvard, who graduated from Emmanuel College at Cambridge University with two degrees, a bachelor's and master's degree of arts.[61] The town of Boston in Lincolnshire furnished many scholars like Rev. Harvard who settled in the New England colonies. According to Walter Moore, out of ninety university men who immigrated to New England, three-fourths of them had graduated from Cambridge University, including Rev. John Cotton, who entered Trinity College, as well as Emmanuel College. After his studies at Emmanuel College, he became a fellow and tutor. He was initiated in the doctrine of Puritanism under the auspices of William Perkins, a Puritan preacher at Saint Mary's.[62]

John Winthrop, Jr., the son of Governor John Winthrop of Massachusetts, was born in Groton Manor, like his father. According to Frederic Calvin Norton, Winthrop Jr. entered Trinity College in England. He also frequented the Inner Temple, where he studied law.[63] Like his son, Governor John Winthrop was also an educated English man. He attended Cambridge University, where he matriculated at Trinity College but did not complete his education.[64] From the same university, we found that Rev. Francis Higginson frequented Jesus College.[65] The list of college graduates who immigrated to New England is long, but we have included these few to give our readers an idea of the New England college graduates or those who had some college education.

John Eliot was also a college graduate, as recorded in various documents in New England. Frederick Norton tells us that he was a student at Jesus College in Cambridge. This was an ancient school that started as a monastery and was a religious house for scholars. In 1496, John Alcock, the Bishop of Ely, received a license from King Henry VII to change this monastery to a college, which, according to G. Dyers, was dedicated to the honor of the Holy Trinity, the Blessed Virgin, and Saint Radegundis of Jesus.[66] In regard to John Alcock, the founder of Jesus College, G. Dyers says that he was born at Beverly in Yorkshire, and attended Cambridge University, where he graduated with a doctorate in 1461. Upon finishing his education, the bishop of London did patronize him. In the same year he finished his education, he was appointed dean of Saint Stephen's Westminster, and he also served Master of the Rolls. In 1472, he was appointed bishop of Rochester. Then, in 1476, he became president of Wales.[67]

Next, there was Thomas Hooker, who was also a clergyman who graduated from Emmanuel College at Cambridge University. Before his studies at Cambridge, he took his university's preparatory training at Market Bosworth. At the end of his university studies, he was appointed rector at the small parish of Ester in Surrey. His salary at that time was forty pounds, which was collected from donations. In 1626, he was a lecturer at Saint Mary's Church at Chelmsford in Essex. At Essex, he was profoundly involved in the teaching of Puritanism. In 1629, he was subjected to the prosecution of Bishop William Laud. Rev. Hooker was born at Marfield in Leicestershire in England on July

7, 1586.[68] Emmanuel College was a Puritan school, from which many prominent clergy of that time graduated. This school was founded in 1584 by Sir Walter Mildmay, a descendant of the Earls of Westmoreland. Sir Mildmay was well connected in the kingdom of England. He served many kings during his years of service. He was entrusted with important offices in the reigns of Henry VIII, Edward VI, Mary, and Elizabeth. He held the position of chancellor of the exchequer. During the reign of Mary, Queen of Scots, he was dispatched in diplomatic missions for many negotiations, and he was deeply involved in Puritanism.[69] In regard to the Puritan studies at Cambridge, John William and Edward Conybeare write that Cambridge University was animated with Protestant ideas. The new theology instituted in that university led to rebellious religious interpretation of the Bible by students.[70] In their views, students who entered this university were antagonistic to the traditional methods of religion. The perceptions of William and Conybeare are true because various clergy members from Cambridge University were prosecuted by Bishop William Laud and his successors.

Rev. John White attended New College, Oxford, and he served as a rector of Trinity Parish in Dorchester for almost forty years. Rev. White has been credited by many writers as one of the architects of the New England colonization movement. He was adamant for this plan and promoted it until the colony was founded. His first plan for the colonization of New England was to establish a fishery settlement. As early as 1623, he was associated with other people in his county for the support of colonization design. To accomplish this, he collected £3,000 sterling, which he reserved from the planting of a settlement on the shores of New England. In addition to fishing prospects, he also believed that such a settlement had to be a free community where inhabitants could express their religious and political views without being subjected to persecution. As such, he communicated with Roger Conant, another noted minister, to establish a settlement in New England.[71]

In the New England colonies, many jurists were also among the Founding Fathers. In the colonies of Massachusetts, Rhode Island, and Connecticut, we discovered names of leading men who acted as lawyers in their home country. In Rhode Island, Roger Williams is on such noted lawyer. He was instructed under the leadership of Sir Edward Coke. In

Massachusetts, Richard Bellingham has been credited for his contributions to the codification of the laws of that colony. He was involved in various processes in the framing, analysis, examination, and codification of the colony's laws. Prior to his migration to New England, he studied law in his country. According to Walter Moore, Richard Bellingham was a recorder in Boston, Lincolnshire, in England from 1623 to 1633.[72] Jacob Bailey Moore says that Bellingham was elected as governor of Massachusetts under the first Massachusetts Charter. He came to New England in 1634 from Boston, Lincolnshire, in England. In the colony, he was praised as a man of good judgment and integrity.[73]

William Douglass, a New England historian, commented on the work of Richard Bellingham for the colony. At the time of his writing, Governor Bellingham was already deceased. He stated that Bellingham had been elected to the position of governor for seven successive years. Before his winning those elections, he had served as assistant or magistrate in the colony, and he also served as the treasurer of the Massachusetts Bay Colony. Douglass went on to note how Bellingham disliked Quakers.[74] Like the previous authors, George Fairbanks Partridge—author of the *History of the Town of Bellingham, Massachusetts*—portrayed Governor Bellingham as a man from a good family. According to his writing, he helped draw up the Charter of the New Massachusetts Colony. He also pointed out that he was one of the Bay Company's twenty-six original members. Regarding his contributions within the government, Partridge notes that he contributed extensively as an experienced lawyer.[75]

In Connecticut, William Leete of Dodington in Huntingdonshire was also a lawyer in his native country. He served as a clerk at the Bishop's Court in Cambridge.[76] Names such as Roger Ludlow, Richard Bellingham, and Nathaniel Ward were men of fame, trained in law, who contributed to the enactments of laws that were subsequently used in New England, as well as in the United States. Nathaniel Ward is the architect of the Massachusetts Body of Liberties. In this work, he was assisted by Richard Bellingham. On the other hand, Roger Ludlow, an imminent jurist, framed the Blue Laws of the Connecticut Colony. According to many writers, Cotton Mather gave important input on the Blue Laws of Connecticut. Roger Ludlow replicated some laws from the Massachusetts Body of Liberties. The Massachusetts laws framed by Nathaniel Ward were composed of the Common Law of England, customary laws, and the Magna Carta articles. These laws were legal instruments utilized for the adjudication of cases, control of citizens' behavior, business regulations, and religious affairs. In addition to jurists, wealthy English people were among the first settlers in New England.

The architecture of the New England colonization movement was supported by influential and wealthy English subjects. Among such people was Richard Saltonstall, of London, who was a wealthy man and the son of the lord mayor of London in 1598.[77] Data from the collection of the Massachusetts Historical Society indicated that the mayor of London, Richard Saltonstall, was his uncle. In the *Calendar of State Papers*, in 1630, his name was mentioned as one of the principal undertakers for the planting of the Massachusetts Bay Colony with Governor John Winthrop.[78] Like Sir Saltonstall, Isaac Johnson was also a wealthy and influential man among those who traveled to Massachusetts with Governor John Winthrop. Johnson contributed unconditionally to the Massachusetts Bay Company. Like other well-off men noted previously, John Hayne was also from a wealthy family. He was an admirer of Hooker and came to America with him. Furthermore, Edward Hopkins, a wealthy Englishman from Shrewsbury, immigrated to New England. He was a merchant and held his headquarters in London. Among these wealthy people were merchants and traders of medium income levels. Even though the New England movement was supported by lawyers, wealthy men, and influential people, religious men were also included in that project.

Like other wealthy Massachusetts Bay Company associates, Matthew Cradock is noted for his unconditional support for the success of the company in England, as well as in the colony. According to various New England historians, he was elected as the first governor of the company in England. When the company's office was transferred to the colony, he remained in England, where he continued his commercial enterprise. Even though he did not immigrate to New England, he dispatched his servants and agents to the newly established colony. According to Charles Brooks, author of the *History of Medford, Middlesex County, Massachusetts,* the agent and servants of Governor Cradock were under the care of Governor John Winthrop. He also stated that Governor Winthrop selected an area where Cradock's farm was to be planted. Brooks writes that Governor Winthrop selected an area at the Mystic River near his own plantation. With respect to his status, Brooks says that he was the wealthiest member of the New England Company.[79]

Like other supporters of the New England movement, religious leaders played a significant role in the success, planning, and settling process in the colonies. In 1629, Rev. John White of Dorchester was profoundly interested in the planting of a fishing post in Massachusetts. As such, he dispatched Dorchester men to New England for that purpose. As early as 1623, he joined the adventures and his countrymen with a plan to make a settlement on the shore of New England. In addition to fishing, he also advocated the establishment of a community in New England where persecuted religious and political victims could find freedom to practice their beliefs. He is proclaimed as the first pioneer who dreamed of the planting of a settlement in New England. In addition to Rev. White, Thomas Hooker of Braintree in Essex County deserves mention. This graduate from Emmanuel College contributed largely to the success and improvement of the Massachusetts Colony, along with Rev. John Cotton.

CHAPTER 4

Pioneers and the Colonization of Connecticut, Rhode Island, and Long Island

The advocacy for colonization of New England territories was also orchestrated by the inhabitants of the colonies of Massachusetts Bay and Plymouth. Many colonies in North America originated from those settlements.[1] In New England, the colonists of Connecticut, Rhode Island, and New Hampshire were first settled in the Massachusetts Bay Colony. This account is recorded in the *Public Records of the Colony of Connecticut*. In this document, data indicate that on April 26, 1636, the magistrates of Connecticut were appointed by Governor Winthrop.[2] The appointment of the Connecticut commissioners by Governor Winthrop signifies the dependency of the colony under Massachusetts Bay. In *The Public Statute Laws of the State of Connecticut*, the colony of Connecticut was recorded as being originally a colony of Massachusetts.[3]

In addition to establishing colonies, records also reveal that inhabitants of Massachusetts Bay and New Haven settled in Long Island, where they built towns such as Southampton, Southold, and Gravesend. English settlers in Southampton migrated from the colony at Massachusetts Bay, especially from Lynn.[4] Like in Southampton, in Gravesend, the inhabitants of Lynn, Massachusetts, were early settlers. According to Alonzo Lewis, Lady Deborah Moody (or Moodey) was one of the pioneers of the migration movement to Long Island. As to her arrival to New England, Lewis notes that she came to Lynn in 1640. Upon her arrival, she was accepted as a member of the Salem Church. Following the norms at the time, -on May 13, 1640-, she was granted four hundred acres of land.[5] She also purchased the farm of John Humphrey, which was located at the place called Swampscot, for the value of £1,100. Due to her religious beliefs, especially her refusal of the baptism of children, she was excommunicated from the church of Salem. As a result, in 1643, she moved to Long Island.[6] Historically, the English in New Amsterdam were from the New England colonies. Benjamin F. Thompson writes that "King's County, unlike other counties was settled by English people, mostly from Massachusetts."[7] As Massachusetts settlers, Rev. Epher Whitaker writes that New Haven inhabitants, under the leadership of Rev. John Youngs, moved to Long Island, where they established the town of Southold.[8] It appears that inhabitants of Massachusetts Bay also settled in Southold. Whitaker records that John Cooper, before moving to New Haven, resided in Boston. After his residency in New Haven, he moved to Southold. He was a wealthy and influential person in Southold and Southampton.[9] Matthias Corwin was also a Massachusetts man from Ipswich who moved to Southold. John Conklin was in Salem before his departure to Long Island.[10] Before 1664, Englishmen resided in Southold, Southampton, and East Hampton. These towns were located on the eastern end of Long Island.[11]

Various documents revealed that dissatisfied planters in Massachusetts Bay always moved to a region of their choice.[12] A good example of this is Roger Ludlow, who came from Western England with Edward Rossiter, John Maverick, and Rev. John Warham.[13] Due to his disappointment of the election of 1635, he moved to Connecticut, where he was an early settler in Watertown and among the leading men of that city.[14] Pertaining to Ludlow, the Dorchester Antiquarian and Historical Society documents that he wanted to be elected governor of Massachusetts Bay. When Governor Haynes was elected instead, he railed loudly against it.[15] It seems that due to his election defeat, he followed Dorchester inhabitants who immigrated to Connecticut. More about Ludlow will be discussed later in this chapter.

New England historians note that there existed discontent among the inhabitants of Massachusetts Bay, due to land or tax concerns. Pertaining to taxes, Governor Winthrop writes about an incident that upset the inhabitants of Watertown. In his book, *The History of New England*, Winthrop records that Watertown inhabitants refused to pay taxes the general court levied for the fortification of the town. As an explanation for the denial, the inhabitants of Watertown refused to pay in such conditions that put them and their posterity into bondage. In addition to that, they claimed the governor and the council in Massachusetts had the same power as the mayor and the alderman. They did not have the power to make laws or raise taxes.[16]

As early as 1633, settlers in Newtown made a complaint to the general court stating that they desired to move to a different area. According to Governor Winthrop, the request was granted. Consequently, they were authorized to survey Agawan and Merrimack as locations to which they had to move.[17] In the same year, Governor Winthrop informs us that John Oldham, accompanied by three associates, visited Connecticut as a trader. During his trip, Oldham was received kindly by Native Americans, who gave him a quantity of beaver. He also purchased hemp, which was in abundance in that region. According to his estimate, Connecticut was about 160 miles from Massachusetts Bay.[18] In this context, it is safe to posit that Oldham's trip triggered malcontent among settlers in Massachusetts who had planned to move to new areas. As a result, they chose Connecticut, which was near their settlements and fruitful for their designs. The abundance of hemp in Connecticut was an indication that land was fertile. In 1634, six settlers in Newtown visited the Dutch plantation in Connecticut with the intent to explore the Connecticut River and settle there.[19] In 1634, during the general court's meeting, the main business discussed was the migration of Newtown settlers. Governor Winthrop notes that removal of the Newtown settlers caused adjournment, and most of time was spent discussing the matter. Accordingly, members of the general court confirmed to allow the Newtown inhabitants to settle other parts of Massachusetts Bay. In the same meeting, deputies agreed that moving to Connecticut was not an issue. During the discussion, the reasons for their removal were also stated and were taken into consideration by some members.[20] At the end of their meeting, members of the general court were divided in regard to the removal of Newtown people to Connecticut. Upon voting, fifteen deputies were for their departure, and ten were against it. Similarly, many assistants were also against the removal of Newtown's settlers to Connecticut. On the other hand, the governor and two assistants favored their removal to Connecticut.[21]

In 1635, an influx of Massachusetts Bay settlers migrated to Connecticut. According to Governor Winthrop, the inhabitants from Dorchester settled near the Plymouth trading house in Connecticut. This act did not please Governor Bradford, who complained to them by mail. After careful consideration and discussion, the matter was solved amicably. The arrival of the Massachusetts Bay men to Connecticut was also recorded by Governor William Bradford. The Plymouth governor writes that Massachusetts Bay men who heard about the richness of the land in Connecticut began planning to settle in that land. It seems that Dutch settlers in Connecticut were opposed to the Dorchester men and those who settled there before them, as noted by Governor Bradford.[22] On July 6, 1635, Governor Bradford received a letter from Johnathan Brewster informing him of the daily arrival of Massachusetts Bay men to Connecticut. The Bay people were recommended to him by Pinchon. Brewster, who was at the Plymouth trading house in Connecticut at the time the Bay people arrived, recalled accommodating twelve men for nine days in Connecticut.[23]

The Connecticut migration movement in Massachusetts Bay was supported by religious ministers such as Rev. John Warham in Dorchester. According to the Dorchester Antiquarian and Historical Society, Rev. John Warham immigrated to Connecticut with the majority of his church members. Rev. Warham had first immigrated to the colony at Massachusetts Bay in 1630, accompanied by inhabitants of western counties in England. After residing for almost five years and few months, he decided to move to Connecticut.[24] His departure to Connecticut with a large portion of the inhabitants of Dorchester was detrimental to the city. The Dorchester Antiquarian and Historical Society documented that newly arrived intelligent and wealthy English settlers left with Rev. Warham to Connecticut.[25] Among the intelligent inhabitants of Dorchester who went to Connecticut was Henry Wolcott. The Dorchester Antiquarian and Historical Society described him as a rich man of superior ability. He was a grantee of lands in Dorchester in April 1633. He also held the position of selectman in 1634. In 1636, he moved to Connecticut. The Dorchester Antiquarian and Historical Society identified him as one of the earliest pioneers of the Connecticut migration movement.[26] Before the departure of Wolcott to Connecticut, in 1635, Nathaniel Gillett and others were the first Dorchester inhabitants who settled Windsor, Connecticut. On the other hand, William Hayden, a man of Dorchester, Massachusetts, moved to Hartford before settling in Windsor in 1642. In addition to the earlier Dorchester settlers, new settlers from London were also advocates of the Connecticut migration movement. Upon their arrival in Dorchester, the new settlers from London financially supported Dorchester settlers traveling to Connecticut. Due to their influence, Dorchester was again deprived of its valuable inhabitants.[27]

Similarly, newcomers from England also orchestrated their own colonial schemes in the territories that were not under the jurisdiction of the Plymouth Colony or the Massachusetts Bay Colony. In 1635, historical data indicate that John Winthrop, the son of the governor of Massachusetts, was commissioned by Lords Saye and Brooke to establish a plantation in Connecticut. In the same way, Richard Saltonstall dispatched his people to take possession of land in Connecticut on his behalf. In the same year, a boat was sent by Governor Winthrop's son to Connecticut. According to Governor Winthrop of Massachusetts Bay, thirty people with provisions were sent to the mouth of the Connecticut River by his son.[28] In 1636, Theophilus Eaton, John Davenport, and others established a colony in New Haven after a temporary stay in Massachusetts Bay and Connecticut. Native Americans called this land Quinnipiac.[29] Eaton was a wealthy merchant and a former statesman in England who served at the Court of Denmark.[30]

Additionally, banished religious leaders from the colony of Massachusetts Bay established their own colonies in New England. This was the case of Roger Williams, William Coddington, John Clarke, and Samuel Gorton.[31] These ministers were banished due to their insistence on freedom of conscience and religious beliefs. Before being banished, these ministers resided in the Massachusetts Bay Colony. Roger Williams was a minister in Salem and afterward moved to Plymouth. Like Williams, Coddington lived in Massachusetts and Plymouth. Gorton was from London and immigrated to Boston, Massachusetts, in 1636. After his stay in Boston, he went to Plymouth. Gorton was a preacher and founder of a religious sect. According to Oliver Payson Fuller, Gorton's political and religious views were antagonistic to the officials and ministers of the Massachusetts Bay Colony.[32] Edgar Mayhew Bacon also noted the conflicting views of Gorton. According to Mayhew, when Gorton visited Providence, he did not reconcile with Roger Williams, due to his political views. He lamented that the government set forth in Providence by Roger Williams was not viable, because it was not initiated by the order of the English Parliament.[33]

With respect to Roger Williams, historians note that he was the founder of Providence Plantation, the first colony in Rhode Island. William Coddington, Dr. John Clarke, and their associates founded Newport, like Roger Williams had done at Providence. On the other hand, Samuel Gorton founded the city of Warwick, with the assistance of his eleven companions. Like Gorton and other ministers, John Oldham, a former settler of the Plymouth Colony, was among Connecticut's pioneers of the colonization movement.

With respect to disgruntled settlers, data shows that Cambridge settlers moved from the Massachusetts Bay Colony and established settlements on the Connecticut River. According to Thomas Spencer Baynes, Rev. Thomas Hooker and his entire congregation founded Hartford, Connecticut. Isaac William Stuart notes that in 1636, Rev. Hooker had with him about one hundred men, women, and children when he traveled to Connecticut.[34] In addition to Rev. Hooker, John Haynes, a former Massachusetts Bay governor, also moved to Connecticut, where he styled himself as one of the founders of that colony. He was the first governor of Connecticut when the three cities of Connecticut formed a single government. Governor Haynes was a wealthy person from Hertford in England. His father was also a landowner in Essex and Hertford counties.[35] Like Governor Hayes, Rev. John Cotton was also among the Massachusetts settlers who moved to Connecticut. According to Frederick Calvin Norton, it was in 1633 that he went to Hartford, Connecticut.

Similarly, Watertown settlers who moved to Connecticut established the town of Wethersfield. Like the settlers from Cambridge and Watertown, the inhabitants from Dorchester founded Windsor. Among the founders of Windsor were Roger Ludlow and Major John Mason, who arrived first in Massachusetts in 1630. After a few years of residence in that colony, Ludlow and Mason moved to Connecticut in 1635. Ludlow was accompanied by settlers from Dorchester. Even though he agreed to travel to Connecticut, at the beginning he objected to the migration of his church members. At the time, he was one of the assistants and the leader of the Dorchester people. Historians write that he objected to such plans because he desired to be elected governor of the Massachusetts Bay Colony. Upon losing the governorship, he was dissatisfied by the choice of Haynes as governor of Massachusetts. According to Henry R. Stiles, inhabitants of Dorchester who founded the town of Windsor were by and large from western English counties. They arrived in New England in 1629. Like other people from Massachusetts, inhabitants from Watertown established the town of Wethersfield in 1634. From the Connecticut towns listed previously, other towns were born, as was the colony of New Haven.

In 1636, Lord Saye and Sele, accompanied by Thomas Welles, came to New England and established a town that they called Saybrook. Like Welles, George Fenwick, a representative of Lords Saye and Sele, and Brooke, came with his family to Saybrook to make a plantation. He named his plantation Saybrook as recognition of the contributions of his bosses, Lords Saye and Sele, and Brooke. Palfrey notes that Lords Saye and Sele, and Brooke were entrepreneurial. With respect to New Haven, this colony was established by wealthy and educated men from London. According to John Gorham Palfrey, Theophilus Eaton, one of the founders of New Haven Colony, was a member and one of the assistants of the Massachusetts Bay Company. It is sound to note that, due to his connection to the Massachusetts Bay Company, their design for the foundation of New Haven Colony was not disputed by the Massachusetts Puritan leaders. In his colonization design, Eaton was accompanied by his friends Rev. John Davenport, Samuel Eaton, and Peter Prudden. In addition to them, Edward Hopkins, a London merchant, was also one of the founders of New Haven Colony.

In 1637, Rev. John Davenport and Theophilus Eaton came to Boston, Massachusetts. After few a months of residence in that colony, they went to Hartford, Connecticut. Like other English settlers, they traveled to Quinnipiac, where they built New Haven Colony. These two leaders were both the principal architects of the political, legal, and economic design of New Haven Colony. Rev. Davenport made an important impact on the establishment of the Connecticut colonial legal system, leading them to incorporate the Mosaic Code into the colony's constitution.

Chapter 5

Lawmakers and the Promulgation of Laws

In colonial New England, the spirit and the letter of law were valued as they were in England and Germany. When English men immigrated to New England, they brought with them the common law and judicial processes (including the various methods of examining evidence) of England. Among the colonists, there were many talented and experienced men in law, who made important contributions in the field of law. With such legal scholars, colonial officials were equipped in examining, revising, appealing, and elaborating new laws for the welfare of the colonies. This was true in the colonies of Massachusetts, Connecticut, New Haven, and Rhode Island. In them, among English immigrants, there were lawyers, jurists, and legal scholars such as Roger Ludlow in Connecticut. According to Isaac William Stuart, "Ludlow [was] emphatically the jurisprudent of his day."[1]

In New England, immigrants who had legal backgrounds were often elected as magistrates. In Massachusetts, some magistrates were trained in the Inner Temple, and others practiced law in their mother country. This was the case of Nathaniel Ward, a religious minister who practiced law in England for some years preceding his move to New England. Like Ward, John Winthrop also frequented the Inner Temple and served as a special attorney of the Court of Wards and Liveries. In 1630, he was elected governor of Massachusetts during the general court held in England by the Council of the Massachusetts Bay Company.

Emanuel Downing, the brother-in-law of Governor Winthrop, was a student of law at the Inner Temple in England. Like other judiciary men listed previously, Richard Bellingham was a recorder in the town of Boston, England, from 1625 to 1633. In the *Records of the Company of the Massachusetts Bay in New England*, he was listed as lawyer, deputy governor, and governor. He was identified as a learned man of incorruptible integrity, great firmness, and acknowledged piety.[2] This account from the *Records of the Company of Massachusetts Bay* pertaining to Governor Richard Bellingham is unquestionable. He labored dearly in establishing good laws in the colony. He was one of the architects of the codification of the Massachusetts Body of Liberties in 1641. At the time when this body of laws was codified, he was the governor of Massachusetts Bay Colony.

Per their charter, which was considered by the colonists to be like a constitution, colonists were permitted to make laws that were not repugnant to the laws of England. As for Plymouth Pilgrims, they devised and agreed to use the Mayflower Compact to govern their colony. In a like manner, the Massachusetts Bay Company was entrusted with the power to make laws by the Council of New England. On March 4, 1629, agents of the Massachusetts Bay Company, in accordance with the language of the charter, determined the number of lawmakers for their business entity. In addition, the shareholders of Massachusetts Bay Company were empowered with executive, legislative, and judiciary power. In the same context of lawmaking, documents reveal that the Massachusetts Bay Company instructed Captain Endecott how to elaborate laws in the plantation of Salem.[3] To better govern the plantation, Massachusetts Bay's officials in England ordered Endecott to observe the laws of England. They also authorized him to inflict punishment on law violators in accordance with the laws of England. Furthermore, he was instructed to empower the head of each family with social control duties. The company allowed him to appoint heads of the family to assist with the control of disorder. In this context, the company advocated preventive measures to avoid destruction of the plantation. To avoid the same, Endecott was advised to employ people under his jurisdiction. According to the company, if servants were employed, they were more likely to become productive and well behaved. As such, young people would imitate the same working behaviors as the adults.[4] The instructions from the company's headquarters in England revealed their lawmaking power. It was the first time that we found laws regulating the company's management in New England.

In Connecticut and New Haven, Massachusetts's legislative procedures were also observed. In these colonies, governors, deputy governors, and assistants were entrusted with legislative power. In 1640, when the towns of Newport and Portsmouth were unified, the Massachusetts Bay style of governing was introduced in the colony of William Coddington.[5] In this year, the titles of governor, deputy governor, assistants, and magistrates were introduced in Rhode Island. Before the introduction of these titles, the judge was the executive administrator of the colony. In 1638, William Coddington was elected as judge in Rhode Island.[6] The freemen of the Rhode Island Colony were organized into a body politic.[7] In the same year, William Aspinwall was elected secretary of the colony.[8] Regarding legislative power, *The Records of the Colony of Rhode Island and Providence Plantations* reveals that laws were framed by the judge with the assistance of men selected by the elders.[9] With such power and responsibilities entrusted to them, the judge and elders were required to assemble quarterly with the mission to review cases and to enact new rules.[10] Among the elders cited in the *Records of Rhode Island* were Nicholas Easton, Mr. John Coggeshall, and William Brenton. They were the elders responsible for choosing the authorities who assisted the judge in formulating and executing laws.[11] On August 1, 1640, the judge and elders were ordered to hear cases together.[12]

Contrary to the practices of the colonies discussed previously, in Providence Plantation, lawmaking methods varied to some extent. Information from the *Records of the Rhode Island and Providence Plantations, in New England: 1636–1663* shows that the colony of Roger Williams did not organize a government. This document did not reveal any settled methods of framing laws. It is sound to note that in Providence, Roger Williams and his associates, including freemen, were involved in the process of elaborating laws. In Providence, the government was incorporated as a town fellowship.[13] In the town of Warwick, Samuel Gorton, the founder and civic leader, did not reconcile with Providence Plantation and Rhode Island Colony because they were not chartered by the crown of England. In his view, the colonies founded by Roger Williams and William Coddington were illegal and did not have the right to exist. In his opinion, as the government formed by

Williams and Coddington did not have the approval of the king or
the Parliament in England, that government did not have the right to
exist.[14] With such perception, he did not form a government or enact
laws for the governing of his colony until 1647, when the unified Rhode
Island colonies formed a government. The original towns—Providence,
Portsmouth, Newport, and Warwick—were unified in 1643 by the charter obtained by Roger Williams from King Charles I. The charter was
named the Incorporation of Providence Plantations in the Narragansett
Bay in New England. In regard to making laws, Dr. John Clarke noted
that before their unification with Providence, and Warwick, "it is in the
power of the body of freemen orderly assembled, or the major part of
them, to make or constitute just laws, by which they will be regulated,
and to depute from among themselves such ministers as shall see them
executed between man and man."[15] Upon arriving in the colony, settlers
with judiciary knowledge were appointed as magistrates or assistants.
Additionally, church ministers were also entrusted with the same power.
To illustrate this, in 1633 in Massachusetts, church ministers were involved during the preparation of the code of laws. Like in Massachusetts,
in Plymouth, Connecticut, New Hampshire, New Haven, and Rhode
Island, ministers were always consulted in the legislative process. In 1639,
ministers were among those empowered to establish courts and frame
laws for the colony. Among them was Rev. Thomas Hooker. He was one
of the framers of the Connecticut Constitution in 1639. Various historians credit his contributions in the framing of the Connecticut Constitution. Accordingly, they note that the expression of the Connecticut
Constitution of 1639 was also later adopted in the United States Constitution by President Thomas Jefferson. Like Rev. Hooker, Rev. Cotton
was involved in the establishment of Connecticut. Before 1639, Roger
Ludlow and seven of his associates were invested with legislative and
judiciary power in the plantations. Likewise, inhabitants in the plantations entrusted them with governance.[16] Thus, there is a probability that
freemen on Connecticut plantations conducted the meetings as they had
when they lived in the Massachusetts Bay Colony.

Just like the Connecticut framers of the laws, in Rhode Island, John
Clarke was also one of the framers of the Rhode Island laws at the
early stage of the colony. In the colonies listed previously, the clergy had

much control over the regulations, framing, and execution of laws. Like Roger Williams, John Clarke was also entrusted with the elaboration of laws for the colony of Rhode Island.[17]

In 1639, in the Massachusetts Bay Colony, the General Court ordered that the laws composed by Rev. Nathaniel be codified. In the same order, the court requested that a committee be charged with examining these laws. Upon finishing their work, copies were sent to several towns so that the church elders and the freemen could examine them. Upon their consideration, the body of laws was finally adopted during the next General Court meeting, which happened on December 10, 1641. The approved body of laws was termed the Body of Liberties. The Body of Liberties resulted from the opposition between freemen and the magistrates, who consolidated excessive power. As a result, deputies claimed that a positive law was needed to diminish the abuse of power by the magistrates.

Governor Winthrop stated in his book *The History of New England* that in 1635, the freemen were discontented about the power of the magistrates, who decided many cases through discretionary power. For that reason, the freemen desired that written laws be codified for the use of the magistrates during court proceedings. About the laws, Governor Winthrop writes that,

> having conceived great danger to our state in regard that our magistrates, for want of positive laws, in many cases, might proceed according to their discretion, it was agreed that some men should be appointed to frame a body of grounds of laws, in resemblance to a Magna Carta, which being allowed by some of the ministers and the General Court should be received for fundamental laws.[18]

This was the first opposition we find regarding the abuse of power by magistrates in the Massachusetts Bay Colony.

As noted by order of the court, Rev. Nathaniel Ward and John Cotton were charged with drafting a body of laws. During this period, Rev. Cotton was a pastor in Boston, Massachusetts. On the other hand, Rev. Nathaniel Ward was a pastor in Agawam, or Ipswich, who was also trained in common law.[19] These two pastors elaborated bodies of laws separately. At the end of their commissions, the copy of laws made by Rev. Ward was approved and codified after their examination by freemen in the colony. The body of laws formed by Rev. Cotton was based on the laws of Moses as recorded in the Old Testament.

In the same year, freemen in this colony were empowered with the enactment of laws for their respective towns. According to the *Harvard Classics*, freemen of each town had control of their judicial institutions and were authorized to enact local laws. It is important to note that freemen's legislative power did not cover criminal matters, only civil actions. The law also entrusted freemen with the power of penalizing law violators with fines under twenty shillings.[20] The language of this law was codified in the Body of Liberties, Article 66.

Lawmaking Organs

It is important to note that in the New England colonies, the general court, the court of assistants, committees, and council were organs empowered with the framing, examination, repeal, and enforcement of laws. *The Records of the Court of Assistants in Massachusetts Bay* reveal that the Court of Assistants was composed of magistrates with legislative power. The same records indicate that at the Court of Assistants of May 18, 1629, and that of August 23, 1630, magistrates were entrusted with executive and legislative power as authorized by the charter.[21] In the same *Records of Assistants*, we discovered that executive and legislative members of the Court of Assistants continued for some years.[22] In 1630 and 1631, the Court of Assistants enacted few laws for the better ordering of the plantations. From the records of the same year, evidence shows that the salary of ministers and wages of servants and government officials, including price controls, were regulated according to the orders of the Court of Assistants.[23] Wage garnishment was also managed according to the order of the court. This will be discussed in the chapter dealing with wage control and employment.

One of the magistrates of this era was William Coddington, the founder of Rhode Island. Like Coddington, Haynes, the founder of Connecticut, was also a magistrate in the Massachusetts Bay Colony.

In 1900, William Thomas Davis writes that the Court of Assistants was formed of the governor and assistants. In regard to the Court of Assistants, Thomas Hutchinson, former Massachusetts governor and historian, notes that this organ was instituted about two months after their arrival in the colony.[24] According to him, the Massachusetts Bay Company's officials assembled for their Court of Assistants meeting in Charlestown. During the Charlestown meeting, a beadle (cooperation officer) was appointed. In the same assembly, the governor and his deputy were entrusted with the duties of the justices of the peace.[25] The power of the Court of Assistants as lawmakers and executive officers was noted by Thomas Hutchinson. He complained that legislative and executive power held by the Court of Assistants violated the charter.[26] Among those who served in the Court of Assistants was Governor Winthrop. Along with the governor, four assistants were also assigned the same duties. Among these assistants in 1629 and 1630 were Richard Bellingham and Roger Ludlow. Moreover, the general court had the same legislative power as the court of assistants. In Massachusetts Bay, assistants were elected by freemen. After their election, assistants were entrusted with the election of the governor and his deputy. In Connecticut, the same law-framing organs were initiated.

The *Public Records of the Colony of Connecticut* indicate clearly that the General Assemblies or Courts were judicial and executive organs of law. In September 1638, the general court in Connecticut was vested with the power of making laws and the organization of other public events. In the same year, we discovered that the general court was divided into two courts, which were convened on different dates. The first court, which was called the Court of Election, was organized on the second Thursday in April. On this occasion, the yearly elections of government officials such as magistrates, the governor, and others were organized. The general court, which was convened in September, was purely a judicial body. In the same *Public Records of Connecticut*, the general courts were described as the supreme power of the commonwealth, and they only had the power to make laws, repeal, to grant land, to admit freemen, to dispose land, and to call either court or magistrate.[27]

Like in Massachusetts and Connecticut, in Rhode Island, English colonists adopted the same procedure for framing laws. According to

*The Proceedings of the First General Assembly of "the Incorporation of Prov-
idence Plantation,"* in 1647, laws were adopted by the assembly of freemen
who gathered at the meeting. From this meeting, it is noticeable that
the first assembly in Rhode Island was convened during the unification
of Providence, Newport, Portsmouth, and Warwick under the charter
obtained by Roger Williams.[28] The charter obtained by Williams was issued on the name of Robert, Earl of Warwick. In the charter, he was appointed governor-in-chief, a lord, and a lord high admiral of the entire
land where the colony of Rhode Island was located. In addition, King
Charles appointed some associates to assist him with the management
of the territory assigned to him under the Rhode Island charter of 1643.
During this period, the towns that constituted Rhode Island were incorporated under the name of Incorporation of Providence Plantation,
in the Narragansett Bay in New England.[29]

The General Court or General Assembly

This legislative organ traces its origin to the forests of Germany. Historians such as Tacitus and Caesar have written with authority on the
Germanic tribe assemblies. Cornelius Tacitus posits that, in the assemblies of the German tribes, prosecutions of offenses were regulated. In
the same assemblies, chiefs were elected and justice administered.[30] In
addition to the account of Tacitus on the Germanic assemblies, Wolfgang Menzel, a respected German writer, documented authoritative
data on these ancient assemblies. In his work *The History of Germany,
from the Earliest Period to the Present Time*, he writes that ancient Germans solved important affairs at the assemblies of freemen. All affairs
of major importance were decided by the freemen. In the district, the
popular assemblies were presided over by the eldest man present at the
time, and the matter was decided by the majority of freemen.[31] These
liberties and practices were also observed in England and in the New
England colonies. Like their German ancestors, in New England, freemen were obligated to report to the general assembly or court.

The general court was a legislative organ in Massachusetts Bay,
Plymouth, Rhode Island, Connecticut, and New Haven. In relation to
the Massachusetts Bay Company, this organ was always convened in

England before the transfer of the company office to New England. This organ can be also termed a general meeting of the freemen where government affairs were transacted. The history of such meetings can be traced among Germanic tribes. M. Guizot, in his *History of the Origin of Representative Government in Europe*, noted important information about the meetings of German tribes. He posited that in the "General Assembly of ancient Germans nothing was decided without the consent of every freeman. Each individual person possessed and exercised his own personal rights and influence. The influence of the chief was great in the national assemblies."[32] Moreover, Guizot noted that the German assemblies were based on the principle of individual rights and the sovereignty of the multitude.[33] The freedoms of expression and assembly accorded to Germans during the national assembly were the same as those of the Anglo-Saxons in England.

In Britain, like in Germany, Anglo-Saxons observed the same procedure. During their era, the kingdom's affairs, such as wars or the establishment and repealing of laws, were settled at the Witenagemot. This council was convened by the king, government dignitaries, and religious authorities. Similarly, in New England, English imported with them the general gathering procedures in which they solved their differences, enacted and repealed laws, divided lands, and attended to other matters of importance to the company. This meeting was valued by the authorities, and freemen were obligated to attend it. In Germany, Tacitus writes that the German assemblies were affairs of great importance to community members. He went on to relate that the Germans' assemblies were scheduled on a specific day. According to him, the Germans' meetings were conducted either at the new or full moon.[34] At the public assembly, Germans were always armed, and their chief acted according to the laws of their land.[35] Similar to their Germans ancestors, in New England, the general court of each colony was scheduled on a certain date as agreed by all.

On March 28, 1629, at the general court convened in England, laws were enacted for the administration of the Salem Plantation. On this date, the Massachusetts Bay Company enacted a law that

> no wrong or injury be [committed] by any of our people to the natives there. To which purpose are desired you, the Governor,

to advise with the Council in penning of an effectual edict, upon penalty to be inflicted upon such as shall transgress the same; which being done, or desire is the same may be published, to the end that all men make take notice thereof, as also that you send a copy thereof into us the next return of the ships.[36]

This law gives us an idea of the power of the general court in making laws for the company. In a like manner, the method of promulgating laws was set forth. It is important to note that the publication of laws for educational purposes in the colony started with the law of 1629 made for Governor Endecott by the Massachusetts Bay Company officials. As ordered by the Massachusetts Bay Company, the governor and the council were entrusted with lawmaking power in the plantation. Additionally, the governor had executive power.[37] Because the plantation was not populated, it is sound to note that old planters were also subjected to the same laws as newly imported servants.

In Massachusetts Bay, this organ was first convened in Boston on October 19, 1630. At first, the general court was a meeting of the management of the company's affairs.[38] The general court was also held in England when John Winthrop was elected governor of the colony of Massachusetts Bay. In the colony, in 1634, freemen from various plantations and towns were incapable of participating in the general court. As a result, an order was passed declaring that the inhabitants from each plantation or town elect their representatives in the general court. Hutchinson notes that representatives of each plantation or town were given full power to make and establish laws, grant lands, and deal in all matters pertaining to the commonwealth.[39]

Despite the order of the court, it was not until 1636 that representatives were chosen from each town or plantation to present their constituents to the general court. That year, the order of the court stipulated that a town of twenty freemen had to choose two deputies to attend the general court. In towns with less than twenty freemen, one deputy was allowed in the general court. However, no deputies were allowed for towns or plantations inhabited by less than ten freemen. A choice was given to towns or plantations with more than thirty freemen. In these locations, they had the liberty of sending a deputy or not sending one at all.[40] As representatives of the freemen, deputies were entrusted with the powers of making and establishing laws, granting lands, and dealing in all other affairs of the commonwealth. This law was passed in 1636 and was reenacted in 1638 and 1653.[41]

Joseph Willard notes that the representative system in America started in 1634 and still continues into our modern time.[42] Contrary to Willard, data indicate that in 1619, Governor Yeardley of Virginia introduced a legislative process with burgess as the representative of the inhabitants. According to various authors, when Governor Yeardley called a general assembly, the inhabitants of each burg in the colony sent two people as their representatives. In 1621, William Waller Hening reveals that two burgesses were chosen from the inhabitants of every town, hundred, or plantation to serve as their representatives in the general assembly. This body had the power of enacting general laws and orders for the welfare of the colony.[43] In the Massachusetts General Court, *the Charters and General Laws of the Colony and Province of Massachusetts Bay*, we discover that "the general court consisting of magistrates, and deputies, [was] the chief civil power of [the] commonwealth; which only [had] power to raise money and taxes upon the whole country, counsel, making of laws, and matter of judicature."[44] In the same charters, the methods of passing laws for the colony were clearly stated. In 1637, the procedure of passing laws was stipulated as follows:

> no law, order or sentence shall pass, or be accounted an act of this court, without consent of the greater part of the magistrates on the one party, and the greater number of deputies on the other party; but all orders and conclusions that have passed by approbation of magistrates.[45]

This law was also reenacted in 1641, which was also the year the Body of Liberties was codified as the fundamental law of the colony. This law clearly demonstrates how the Puritans valued the notion of the rule of law.

In 1638, in Connecticut, research indicates that each town sent deputies to the general court. For example, in this year, Windsor, Hartford, and Wethersfield all sent deputies.[46] With this title, they became elected officials mandated with the framing of laws for the welfare of the colony. According to Thomas Hutchinson, in 1634, "the general court had the power to make and establish laws, or to elect and appoint officers as governor, deputy governor, assistants, and treasurer." He also pointed out that the general court secretly raised monies and taxes.[47] In addition to this, the court had the power to repeal, revise, and amend framed or elaborated laws. According to the Massachusetts archives, deputies elected from plantations and towns were wealthy men. There is no evidence that poor people were elected as representatives in the general court. In 1644, the assembly was divided into two legislative bodies: the House of Assistants and House of Deputies.[48] These two legislative bodies were entrusted with legislative power.

In 1647, when the Rhode Island towns of Newport, Portsmouth, Providence, and Warwick were united, a government was formed, and a general court was instituted. In this colony, the general court was termed the Court of Commissioners, or later the General Assembly. According to the *Records of the Colony of Rhode Island and Providence Plantations*, this organ was a legislative body.[49] The executive power was vested to the governor, the deputy governor, and the assistants. In 1679, when New Hampshire separated from the colony of Massachusetts, a general assembly was organized in the province. Before this date, the colony of New Hampshire was under the jurisdiction of Massachusetts Bay. From 1641 until 1679, the laws of Massachusetts were observed and enforced in New Hampshire. In 1679, when New Hampshire became a royal province, John Cutt was appointed president of that province. Under the royal province, on March 16, 1678, a general assembly was convened by the freemen of New Hampshire. At this assembly, the General Assembly was officially empowered with the ability to make laws and ordinances for the province. According to Jeremy Belknap, the General Laws and Liberties of the Province of New Hampshire were also enacted during the same assembly.[50]

The Committees

The duties of committees entrusted with the elaboration, examination, revision, and codification of laws and ordinances in New England have been recorded by various historians. To illustrate this, in the *Records of the Governor and Company of Massachusetts Bay*, the duties and names of men who served in the committee for the preparation or revision of laws were recorded. Likewise, Governor John Winthrop records the same in his journals. In the *Public Statute Laws of Connecticut* such information can also be found. The members of the committee entrusted with the framing of laws were knowledgeable of law and the society in which they lived; others were religious people. In many cases, clergy and magistrates were on the committees that framed, revised, examined, or codified laws in the New England colonies.

The history of commissioning lawmakers with certain powers of framing, discussing, reviewing, and appealing laws is not new in the United States. During the colonial period, research reveals that in the New England colonies, honorable, modest, and prominent people were selected to form committees specifically for the duties of framing the laws of the colony. According to the *Records of the Court of Assistants of Massachusetts Bay*, committees were appointed from time to time with the objective of the establishment of drafting of laws.[51] This power was assigned to them in accordance with the law of 1635. On March 7, 1643, Governor Winthrop, Dudley, and Hibbens formed a committee to examine the Body of Liberties.[52] In 1646, according to the *Records of the Court of Assistants of the Massachusetts Bay Colony*, Richard Bellingham and Ward were assigned with the revision of laws. From time to time, a committee was assigned for the revision of laws in the colony of Massachusetts. Among the members of the committee, Richard Bellingham was deeply involved in the legislative process. As a lawyer, he was credited for his laborious duties for that purpose. Upon revising laws, he always returned to the general court for the general revisions of all members of the committee.[53] On November 24, 1654, another committee was entrusted with the preparation of a law for blasphemy. In this committee, the clergy were also given the same power as the other members of the committee.[54]

In October, 1640, research indicates that in Connecticut, George Wyllys, Thomas Wells, and William Spencer were members of the committee tasked with the revision of laws for that colony. This committee was formed of intelligent and reputed men in the colony. Wyllys was an assistant to the general court, Wells was a magistrate, and William Spencer was an intelligent deputy from Hartford.[55] Laws in the colony were revised periodically. As a result, there were many commissions for that end.

In 1671, the governor, the deputy governor, and the majority of the assistants in Connecticut were appointed to revise the laws, as well as arrange them. In these duties, they were assisted by the secretary of state. After the revisions of the law, the secretary was ordered to prepare a draft of the law, which was presented to the general court for final examination and approval.[56] In the same colony, in 1672, Samuel Wyllys and James Richards were entrusted with the inspection of established laws. Other duties delegated to them were to compare the recorded laws with the original copies and to verify if corrections were needed.[57] In Rhode Island, committees were also delegated to enact, review, and examine laws from the other colonies. In New Hampshire, on October 12, 1680, a committee was selected for the establishment of laws as similar as possible to the laws of England. The same laws had to be suitable to the constitution of the province of New Hampshire.

Codification of Laws in the New England Colonies

Before a discussion on the codification of laws in New England, it is essential to discuss this procedure briefly in the kingdom of England, from where the settlers emigrated. It is important to incorporate how Germanic tribes valued liberty and equality. To maintain those values, positive laws were established and codified. Wolfgang Menzel informs us that, in England, Anglo-Saxons kept the Germanic codes with them. These codes were progressively advocated by the kings.[58] Like in Germany and England, in the New England colonies, Pilgrims and Puritans observed the same norms for the codifications of laws as their forefathers. While codifying laws, colonists in New England utilized the same sources as their ancestors. They took into account the common law of England, Mosaic laws, and Christian principles. In England, King Alfred based his code on incorporating Mosaic laws. In Massachusetts Bay, Connecticut, and New Haven, the capital laws were also based on the common law of England and the Magna Carta.[59]

Historically, during the Anglo-Saxon era in England, laws were first codified by King Ethelbert around 591.[60] With the assistance of his Witan, King Ethelbert published his doombook, or code of law. According to George Blaxland, the laws of King Ethelbert were written in Anglo-Saxon. Following his lead, Hlothaire, Eadric, and Wihtraed published their laws in 699 in the kingdom of Kent. In 700, King Ina of Wessex published his laws.[61] Spencer writes that King Ina was the head of the Saxon heptarchy and gave his attention to codifying good laws. It appears that King Alfred followed the example of Ethelbert in codifying laws.[62] These kings codified the laws of the kingdoms under their jurisdictions. During the reign of King Alfred, the common laws of England were codified for the entire realm.[63] As he went about doing this, the kingdom was still under the name of the Saxon heptarchy. Under the reign of Egbert, the Saxon kingdoms were named England after the Anglii. This tribe was in the majority in the kingdom. Egbert has been credited as being the founder of the English monarchy. Egbert spent much of his life in France in exile at the court of Charlemagne, the king of France. According to George Spencer, he lived at the court of Charlemagne for twelve years.[64] Like their Saxon forefathers, colonists in New England observed the same methods regarding the codifying of laws.

In the New England colonies, the administration of laws was entrusted to various leaders in Massachusetts Bay; for example, the governor, lieutenant governor, and deputies were empowered with the enforcement, execution, and framing of the laws of the colony. Moreover, church officials also had the same adjudicative power as the magistrates.[65] These complexities in the judiciary system caused discontent among the inhabitants of the colony. Positive laws were needed to remedy the conflicts between deputies and civil magistrates. As a result, Rev. Nathaniel Ward and Rev. Cotton were assigned with the task of framing a code of law for the colony of Massachusetts Bay. This code was approved by the elders, the leaders of the Massachusetts Bay Company, and the people. In 1641, this law was voted upon, adopted, and named the Massachusetts Body of Liberties. Accordingly, the Body of Liberties was composed of a hundred laws. The Massachusetts code served as the framework for the colonies of Connecticut and New

Hampshire. William H. Whitmore writes that "a thorough consideration of the Body of Liberties will prove that our ancestors were far more enlightened than their English contemporaries, and that their influence which they sent forth has continued to affect most powerfully our laws, customs, and thoughts to the present time."[66] The perception of Whitmore is unquestionable. It is certain that the Massachusetts Body of Liberties had an impact on the laws of Massachusetts, Connecticut, and New Hampshire, as well as the United States Constitution. In addition to the codification of the Body of Liberties, the Massachusetts laws of 1660 and 1672 were also codified.

In 1646, the General Court of Connecticut tasked Roger Ludlow with the codification of the laws of that colony and with presenting them to that body during the next meeting. According to the record from *The Public Statute Laws of Connecticut*, Ludlow did not complete the code as requested by the general court. He continued his work in 1647 and divided the code, modeling the Code of Justinian. Up to 1650, the code was not complete. It was in 1651 that the code of laws prepared by Ludlow came into effect after being approved by the general court. Despite Ludlow's code being finished in 1651, it is always termed the Connecticut Code of 1650. In 1655, in New Haven, the general court asked Governor Eaton to prepare a code of laws for the colony.[67] We did not find any record of the completion of such code. In 1665, the General Court of Connecticut followed the same patterns as the colony of Massachusetts. Early laws established in the colony were not recorded or codified. The general court requested that an able, judicious man form a code of laws for the colony of New Haven. For this purpose, Governor Eaton was appointed. Upon his appointment, he requested the general court to assign him an assistant. Governor Eaton also examined the laws of Massachusetts and selected those that were usable in New Haven. Rev. Cotton was also appointed as an aid to Governor Eaton for the framing of the New Haven code of laws.

The codification of laws in Rhode Island can be traced to 1647 during the incorporations of the towns in that colony. From *Laws and Acts of Her Majesties Colony of Rhode Island and Providence Plantation*, we discovered that a code of law was adopted but was opposed by Francis Brinley, Nathaniel Coddington, and Peleg Sanford. After the objection

of these officials, another attempt was made in 1654. In this year, Ezekiel Holliman and John Green, Jr. were ordered by the general court
to examine the general laws of the colony and report them to the next
general court. It appears that the law was not codified. In 1656, Dr. John
Clarke was also ordered by the General Assembly to assemble the laws
of the colony in a better form and reject those that he found unneces-
sary for the good of the colony. He was also ordered to add new laws
that he thought were important for the regulation of courts.[68] It does
not appear that he completed this mandate. In 1664, the laws of the colony were codified after a revision of the General Assembly.[69]

In 1641, in New Hampshire, the codified Body of Liberties of the
Massachusetts Bay Colony was in effect. Thereafter, the colony was governed under the laws of Massachusetts until 1679, when they were separated. In 1680, a code of law was composed by John Cutt, the president
of the colony. This code is always called the Cutt Code. According to the
New Hampshire Reports, this code of laws was passed in March 1680 by
the General Assembly. In 1682, Edward Cranfield, the lieutenant governor, codified laws, and some of the former acts were modified.[70] Cutt's
Code was composed of many laws from the colony of Massachusetts
Bay, as noted in the Laws of New Hampshire. According to that document, the criminal code of New Hampshire under President Cutt was
adopted almost verbatim.[71] Secretary Chamberlain claimed that Cutt's
laws were collected from the laws of Massachusetts.[72] Enacted laws were
always promulgated in various towns and plantations by orders of the
general court of each colony.

Methods for Promulgating Laws

In the early years of the New England colonies, laws were declared
during town meetings or other assemblies. In addition to this, local officials such as constables were entrusted with the proclamation of laws in
their respective towns, plantations, and counties. The history of assigning
local officials to the proclamation of laws in their local jurisdictions can
be traced to the kingdom of England. According to Sir Edward Coke,
the Status of Winchester was to be published four times yearly and sent
to every county so it could be read.[73] There is no question that the Status

of Winchester was read in towns, counties, and villages. The proclamation of the statute was ordered because many robberies, burnings, and
manslaughters were committed in the realm.[74] It appears that the statute
was not observed by many of the English. Therefore, the king had to enforce it. It is reasonable to speculate that the king wanted everyone in the
realm to have knowledge of the laws regarding robberies, burning, and
manslaughters and the consequences of their violation. In this case, the
proclamation of the statues served to educate the public and deter them
from these crimes. Just as Sir Coke had, T. Cunningham recorded that
during 6 Stat. Ric. 2, Cap. 6 [Act of parliament passed during the reign
of King Richard II.], the proclamation of the Status of Winchester was
under the jurisdiction of the sheriff of every hundred. In a like manner,
the bailiffs of each market town were also entrusted with the proclamation of the Winchester Status in their bailiwick.[75]

In Massachusetts, general marshals were always discharged with
the promulgation of laws. It is important to note that there was no
printing press in Massachusetts Bay or in Plymouth. Like the colonies
of Massachusetts and Plymouth, the colonies of Rhode Island, Connecticut, and New Haven also lacked printing presses. Enacted laws
were recorded in town records and the records of the General Assembly. Upon the adoption of laws, the general court ordered the secretary
of state to make copies and send them to each town. In each town, a
constable was dispatched with instructions regarding the instruction of
laws to the inhabitants. In Connecticut, the constables read the laws
at the public meeting so that each inhabitant had knowledge of the
established laws and punishments for violations. The selectmen were
also entrusted with the publication and transmission of laws. Among
the duties of the selectmen listed in the General Laws of Massachusetts
was the teaching of the capital laws to the children. In 1650, the general
court ordered that a copy of the book of laws be submitted to the clerk
of each court, the deputies of each town, or the constables of each town
where there were no deputies. They were charged with reading this book
at a public meeting within ten days of receiving it. Officials who failed
to meet this requirement were ordered to pay five pounds.[76] From the
Public Statute Laws of Connecticut, we discovered that after an act was

passed in Connecticut, within a limited time, constables ordered that the public statues be written in a book for the town's future use. As there were no printing presses in the colony, constables were obligated to read them yearly in a public meeting.[77] Elizabeth Hibbell Schenck, in *The History of Fairfield, Fairfield County, Connecticut: From the Settlement of the Town in 1639 to 1818,* writes that "at each session of the general court, and once every year, the constables in the several towns, were required to read or cause to read, in some public meeting, all such laws as were then in force."[78]

Local Officials or Councils

It is important to discuss the enactments of laws at the local level. In Massachusetts Bay, Connecticut, and Rhode Island, local officials were entrusted with self-governing power. In 1636, Massachusetts selectmen were permitted by the general court to make laws for the regulations of their various towns' affairs. We discovered that residency requirements were regulated at the town level. In 1636, Boston enacted a law preventing any person from entertaining a visitor above fourteen days.[79] In 1658, Dorchester enacted almost the same law. In Dorchester, the law ordered that "no person shall take anyone into his house without the consent of the selectmen."[80] When the press was established in Massachusetts, laws were printed at Cambridge.

Printed Laws

Record keeping in the United States is a cultural way of life. From their forefathers in England, laws were recorded for the use of future generations. Many records indicate that King Alfred requested the assembling of all laws of England into one body, which has been termed the common law of England. We discovered that many English lawmen, such as Lord Edward Cooke, Blackstone, Palgrave, and others, have recorded salient data on the laws of the realms of England. The laws of rulers such as Alfred, Henry I , John I, Henry I, Henry VIII, and Queen Elizabeth, among others, are accessible in our modern era. Even the laws of Anglo-Saxon kings are easy to collect. Therefore, English in the colonies were well equipped for record keeping. In fact, among them, Richard Bellingham was a record keeper in Boston, England.[81] In regard to court records, in 1632, the Massachusetts General Court declared that 110 records of evidence were kept for the good uses of precedent and posterity. In the same year, the court ordered that the evidence and court's judgment be recorded in a book and kept for posterity.[82] The orders of the general court reveal how the officials of Massachusetts Bay colony valued the court's records and their desire to preserve its precedents for the use of their descendants for years to come.

Like their Anglo-Saxon ancestors, officials in colonial New England ordered the printing and recording of all laws in the colonies for the use of the courts and learning purposes. This approach was healthy for the courts, deputies, and members of the general court. In our modern era, records kept by the colonial secretaries and other officials are beneficial to students, researchers, professors, and scholars. These records have been quoted, interpreted, and analyzed by many historians, legal thinkers, and jurists. Court records, rulings by the general courts, and the laws framed by the colonists in New England could not be printed if the press was not established in the colonies.

In 1639, the first printing press was established in the New England colonies. This press was first instituted by Rev. Jose Glover, who died while returning from England to America. Upon his death, Stephen Daye established a press in Cambridge at Harvard College. His first published work was "The Freeman's Oath." In 1640, he printed the "Bay Psalm Book." Daye was born in England in 1611 and lived in Cambridge, Massachusetts, until his death in 1668. It appears that he came to Massachusetts in 1639 with his master Rev. Jose Glover.[83] With regard to his training as a pressman, little is known. There is no information on how Daye learned how to use printing machines. It is possible that he was trained in England, where the printing press was purchased. In the kingdom of England, the first press was established by William Caxton, who was trained at the Mercers' Company.[84] According to Rev. J. Bosworth, he was also a member of that company. Rev. Bosworth qualified him as a master of the art of printing. In England, the first book printed by Caxton was completed in 1474. As the press was implemented in the kingdom, the University of Cambridge also established its own printer in 1478.[85] Before his printing work in England, Caxton was credited with printing a book in 1471 in Cologne, Germany.[86] The art of printing can be traced to Germany, where Johannes Gutenberg constructed the first printing press. According to some sources, his proper name was Gensfleisch, or Gansfleisch, and he was born in Mainz.[87] Gutenberg probably invented the printer in 1436, when he made a contract with Andrew Dryzehn and printed his wonderful art. This printer was first serviceable around 1438. A few years after Gutenberg returned to Mainz in 1443, he patterned with Johannes Fraust or Fust, who was a wealthy goldsmith at the time.[88] Fraust, a wealthy man, established the first printing press. His first publication was a Latin Bible. It is also important to note that Fraust spent his money on the improvement of the printing machine invented by Gutenberg.[89]

In 1642, the General Court of Massachusetts Bay ordered that laws that made any offense a capital crime should be printed and published. The law ordered the secretary of state to send a copy to the printer. Upon the examination of the first copies by the governor or Richard Bellingham, the treasurer was ordered to pay for the final printing.[90] In the same year, the general court ordered "that every court should have a copy of the laws at the public charge."[91] In the same context, research shows that Richard Bellingham was tasked with composing a book of laws for the colony. In 1646, the general court ordered that the court should refer to the book of laws in their proceedings from time to time.[92] In 1648, research shows that the Massachusetts book of laws was at the press. The price for the book was fixed at three shillings by order of the general court. The court preferred that every member of this body receive a free copy. The court also ordered the auditor general and Joseph Hill to order fifty copies of the book of law.[93]

In 1649, members of the Massachusetts general court were pleased with keeping the book of laws in print format. As a result, they appointed Richard Bellingham and Nowell to prepare a book of former laws and sent it to press.[94] In 1650, the general court ordered that Richard Bellingham and Hills take order of sending the laws to the press for printing purposes.[95] In 1658, the book of code became the law of the colony. In 1672, the general court of Plymouth ordered that the laws of that colony be printed at the Cambridge press located at Harvard College. In 1673, the laws of the colony of Connecticut were printed by Samuel Green.[96] According to *The Public Statute Laws of the State of Connecticut*, the Cambridge press was the first printing press established in North America.

Chapter 6

Employment and Wages
in the New England Colonies

Regulations covering employment and wages in New England have been discussed by many scholars and historians such as Charles Brooks, Isaac William Stuart, William Hubbard, Joseph B. Felt, Alonzo Lewis, John Winthrop, and the Massachusetts Historical Society. Among the authors named previously, Charles Brooks recorded authoritative information on regulatory laws in the town of Medford. In his book *History of the Town of Medford, Middlesex County, Massachusetts*, he noted game, employment, price, dress code, military, school, currency, and wage regulations.[1] In colonial records, as well as the *Records of the Company of Massachusetts Bay*, data reveal laws enacted for the enforcement of wages. In the *Charter and Laws of the Colony and Province of Massachusetts Bay in New England*, laws enacted for wages and the management of employees are discussed. Similarly, pertinent data on wages and employment regulations are recorded in *Records of the Colony and Plantation of New Haven, from 1638 to 1649*. In this work, we discovered that in the winter of 1640, servants worked eight hours a day.[2]

Moreover, in *The Compact with the Charter and Laws of the Colony of New Plymouth*, various acts pertaining to employment laws are mentioned. To illustrate this, in that colony, government officials were prohibited from transferring technological knowledge or service to strangers and to foreigners. The act ordered that

> no handy craftsman of what profession soever as tailors, shoe-makers, carpenters, joiners, smith, sawyers, or whatever which do or may reside or belong to this plantation of Plymouth shall use their science or trades at home or abroad for any strangers

or foreigners till such as the necessity of the colony be served,
without the consent of the governor and council. The breach
thereof to be punished at their discretion.[3]

This act indicates that protectionism was stringently observed
during the time of the Pilgrims and Puritans in New England. In our
modern era, we can assert that President Donald J. Trump's "America
First" policy has a long history in this land.[4]

As noted in the previous chapters, the settlers of New England were
of English stock. As such, they brought with them their ancestors' norms,
mores, cultures, and laws. In England, for centuries, wages were regulated
by laws enacted by kings. During the reign of King Edward III Wages
were regulated in accordance with the Ordinance of Labourers 1349 declared by him, and the Statutes of Labourers of 1351 passed by members
of the parliament.[5] Upon the passage of these statues, the English Parliament fixed the yearly wages for categories of workers.[6] In these same
statutes, the increase of wages was prohibited, and violators were subject
to punishment. Thomas Ruggles notes that

> people were restrained from giving more by pecuniary penal-
> ties. The pain for the violation of these statutes was divided into
> three levels. According to the law, the pain for the first offense for
> the violation of the Statutes of Labourers was the forfeiture of
> the overplus. The second violation was sanctioned by paying the
> double of the overplus and treble the overplus for the third of-
> fence. Sometimes, the third violation of the Statutes of Labourers
> was sanction by being imprisoned for forty days.[7]

During the reign of King Edward III, receiving or giving higher
wages not prescribed by the statutes was punishable.[8] The increase of
wages during the reign of King Edward III resulted from the shortages
of laborers. After the war with France, poor people were no longer
villains or slaves of their lords. As such, they wished to receive better
wages for their work. Contrary to their aims, the law of the kingdom
prohibited the increase of wages at that time.[9] John Reeves, a barrister
at law, notes in his *History of the English Law* that when servants and

laborers discovered that masters had difficulties in recruiting people to work for them, they demanded excessive wages. It appears that those who were not satisfied with the wages refused to work and became beggars. Consequently, wages became subject to regulatory laws and termed the Statutes of Labourers. The enacted statutes stipulated the following:

> every man and woman, able in body, and within the age of three-score, not living in merchandize, nor exercising any craft, not having his own whereof to live, nor land about tillage he might employ himself, nor serving any other, such person should be bound to serve, if required, at the accustomed wages; and if he refused, was to be committed to the next goal, till he found surety to be entered into service, if any workman or servant departed before the term agreed, he was to be imprisoned, c.2.[10]

In the same regulation, masters were also prohibited to pay servants more money as required by law. The labor's regulation declared that "none were to pay more than the old wages, upon pain of forfeiting double what they gave, c.3; and if any took more, he was to be committed to goal, c.5."[11] As it had functioned in England, New England officials acted the same when there were shortages of workers. The increase of wages was prohibited, and it was subject to government regulation.

The same approach regarding high wages was enforced during the reign of King Richard II. On the 12th of Richard II. Cap. 4 [Act of parliament passed on the 12th year of King Richard's reign], giving or taking more wages than settled by statute was punishable. To avoid the punishment, justices of the peace, mayors, and aldermen were entrusted with proclaiming the rate of wages in their respective towns and counties. This was the first time we found that wages were regulated at the local level and at the discretion of local officials.

During the reign of Queen Elizabeth I, a master who paid his servants more wages than fixed by law was imprisoned for ten days. In a similar manner, servants who received more money for their work were imprisoned for twenty-one days.[12] The history of wages in England gives us a clear view of its enforcement in New England. The same provisions and enforcement methods were observed in New England with some modifications. In addition to wages, working periods were regulated by law. During the reign of King Edward III, some workers were employees on a yearly basis or for other negotiated terms, but not on a daily basis.[13]

In 1545, in England, the wages of superior mechanics and sawyers were rated at four pence a day. In addition to wages, they were accommodated with food and drink, which was valued at three pence.[14] In the same kingdom, during the reign of King Henry, an artisan was paid two to three shillings a week. By his regulation, the artisan had to work no more than eight hours a day.[15] From this law, it is pertinent to speculate that the legal daily hours codified in the employment laws in New England can be traced to England. Like in the reigns of the kings listed previously, during the reign of King Henry V, a workman was paid from three pence to sixpence a day.[16] Similarly, we discovered that in the kingdom of England, the hourly paid was observed as in our modern era. Despite the prohibition of working more than eight hours, the statute does not detail the punishment for that provision.

In the New England colonies, the employment of servants and apprentices and their wages were regulated by laws established by the general court, as in England, by the king and the parliament. The *Records of the Massachusetts Bay Company* show that wages for the servants were made off the stock of the company and those of their private partners. According to the Massachusetts Bay officials in England, Governor Endecott had to collect half from the company stock and the other half from private partners for the wages of servants.[17] This was the first mention of wages in the *Records of the Massachusetts Bay Company*, in the Company's Second General Letter on Instructions to Endecott and his Council. The letter was written in London on May 28, 1629. In this letter, many instructions were detailed for the government regarding the enactment of laws, training of servants, and social control methods.[18]

The New England colonies were corporate bodies politic. These colonies were governed by the influential founders and wealthy men. Governing officials in these colonies were lawmakers as well as judiciary officers. They enacted laws for the welfare of the colony and adjudicated cases brought before them. In accordance with the charters issued to them by the kings, they were obligated to enact laws for the better governance of the colonies. Therefore, they were in obligation to enact and promulgate laws that were not contrary to the laws of England. With respect to the enactment of laws, they did not have difficulties, because the colonists had legal backgrounds. As such, they were able to establish laws based on the conditions in the colonies, as well as recourse to the common law of England.

The accounts pertaining to laws governing the management of servants and apprentices have been noted by various historians in New England, as well in other parts of the United States. In New England, colonial authorities left a large amount of information regarding this matter. William Hubbard, in his *History of New England*, documented the control of wages in Massachusetts Bay. Caleb Hopkins Snow documented the same in his book *A History of Boston*. In addition to these authors, William B. Weeden, in his book *Economic and Social History of New England, 1620–1789*, recorded unquestionable data on regulatory laws in the New England colonies, which included the control of wages and prices. In 1844, Alonzo Lewis stated important information about regulatory laws enacted in 1630. His book, titled *The History of Lynn: Including Nahant*, contains instructional data on wages and pricing regulations established in the early years of the Massachusetts Bay Colony. In the *Records of the Court of Assistance of the Colony of the Massachusetts Bay, 1630–1692*, wages and price regulations are recorded.

In 1630, upon the arrival of Massachusetts Bay Colony officials, laws were established for the management of the company, which included regulatory laws. It appears that wages and price control were tackled at the same time. Regarding wages, Alonzo Lewis writes that, in 1630, an order of the general court was passed for the regulation of wages. According to him, the court ordered that "no master carpenter, mason, joiner, or bricklayer was permitted to earn more than 16 d. a day for their daily work if they are provided with food and drink."[19] A bricklayer was not allowed to receive pay of twelve pence a day for his work. Violation of this order was punishable by law."[20]

During the first Court of Assistants held at Charlestown on August 23, 1630, the court ordered that carpenters, joiners, bricklayers, sawyers, and thatchers had to be paid up to two shillings a day. In the same order, it was declared that sawyers shall not be paid more than four shillings and sixpence a day.[21] This order was not productive, and officials had to decriminalize the increase of wages, which was accomplished after few months. On March 22, 1630, at the Court of Assistants at Boston, an order was passed abolishing the punishment for the violations of wage regulation. In this year, workers and employers were permitted to negotiate daily wages at reasonable terms.[22]

In 1631, the Court of Assistants of the colony of Massachusetts enacted orders for the regulation of workmen and other laborers' wages.[23] According to William B. Weeden, the general court and several towns' efforts to enforce and control wages were in vain.[24] Weeden also noted that, in 1634, the fine of five shillings for the violation of wages was repealed. It was also during this year that town officials were entrusted with the regulation of wages in their respective localities. Accordingly, three men were appointed by the town for negotiation when there was a dispute in that matter.[25]

John Winthrop recorded in his journal authoritative data regarding the control of wages and its enforcement. He clearly stated the reason why the increase in wages happened in Massachusetts Bay. He posited that the shortage of workers affected the employment market in the colony. In his journal, Governor Winthrop declared that

> the scarcity of workmen had caused them to raise their wages to an excessive rate, so as a carpenter would have three shillings the day, a laborer two shillings, etc., and accordingly those who had commodities to sell advanced their prices sometimes double to that they cost in England, so as it grew to a general complaint, which the court, taking knowledge of, as also some further evils, which were springing out of the excessive rates of wages, they made an order, that carpenters, masons, etc., should take but two shillings the day, and laborers but eighteen pence, and that no commodity should be sold at above four pence in

ready money in England; oil, wine, etc., and these, in regard of
the hazard of bringing, etc., [excepted].[26]

As the wages increased, complaints were made to the general court.
To remedy this, the general court made an order for the regulation of
wages in the colony. In 1633, the general court fixed the wages of various
categories of workmen. An example, the carpenters and masons were
paid two shillings a day. Laborers had to be paid eighteen pence a day.[27]
Regulation of wages was also another approach to discourage idle workers.[28] It seems that, with the increase of wages, many servants spent
more time doing less work, hoping to gain more money while working
fewer hours a week. In Massachusetts, the regulation of wages was reenacted from time to time. As an illustration of this, in Massachusetts
Bay, wages were regulated in accordance with the laws of the colony in
1630, 1631, 1633, and 1634.

In the colony of Connecticut, wages were also regulated by order
of the court. The *Public Records of the Colony of Connecticut [1636–1776]*
indicate that on June 7, 1641, the general court of that colony con-
demned the excess of wages paid to artificers and workmen. It appears
that wages before the order of the court were discussed between servants and masters. As a result, the general court ordered that carpenters,
plowrights, wheelwrights, masons, joiners, smiths, and coopers had to
receive twenty pence as daily wages from March 10 to October 11. For
the rest of the year, the listed workmen were paid eighteen pence daily
according to the order of the court. The order also legislated the daily
work hours. In the law of 1641, workmen were permitted to work eleven
hours daily in the summer and nine hours in winter.[29] In 1655, the wages
of commissioners were regulated by the act of the Assembly. According
to the *Records of the Colony of Rhode Island and Providence Plantations,
in New England: 1636–1663*, men selected as commissioners by town officials were authorized three shillings daily as wages. In the same order,
failure to serve as commissioner after being selected was punishable.
The fine for this infraction was three shillings daily for the violation for
the benefit of the town. For each violation, the court ordered the forfei-
ture of six shillings a day payable at the court.[30]

In addition to wages, the behavior of servants and apprentices were also legally regulated in the New England colonies. For example, in 1646 in colonial Massachusetts, thefts at work were punishable by a law that declared "that all servants and workmen embezzling, the goods of their masters or such as set them on work, shall make restitution, and penalties as other men."[31] Thefts at the workplace are also punishable by law in the United States. Even though employees engaging in minor theft did not face charges, they were always fired from the company. This type of behavior is unacceptable in the United States. American employers do not tolerate criminal behavior of any kind, without exception. Even stealing time from a company is prohibited by its policies. Contrary to the United States, in the developing countries, illegitimate behavior such as theft at work is tolerable due to the patronage system. In various developing countries, government officials, from time to time, embezzle government funds and property for personal gain.

In the New England colonies, the safety of workers was also taken into consideration by colonial officials. In private industries, employers were ordered to protect their workmen. *The Charters and Laws of Massachusetts Bay* indicates that an act was passed for the regulations of work safety. The acts respecting masters, servants, and laborers were established for the welfare of employers and employees. According to this law, "all workmen shall work the whole day, allowing convenient time for food and rest."[32] From this law, it is sound to note that our modern break time at work is consistent with the colonial laws. Colonists understood that workers needed a break to be productive at work. This law was likely enacted because many masters were not providing rest (break time) for their servants and laborers. To remedy this, the general court was obligated to establish a law for the benefits of masters, servants, and laborers.

In Connecticut, the selectmen were empowered with the arbitration of concerns that arose from employment disputes such as wages and oppression from masters. Isaac William Stuart, in his book *Hartford in the Olden Time: Its First Thirty Years*, records that the selectmen administered oppressions resulting from any overburdened or disproportioned labor done to individuals for the town, and occasioned by the ignorance or corruption of those who supervised workers.[33] Like in Connecticut, the arbitration methods are also observed in various companies in the United States. Human resource officials often settle conflicts between employees or their managers. Open policies, as companies have termed them, are always the best approach to resolving conflicts in the workplace in the United States.

Wages for Government Officials

In colonial New England, government officials were paid according to the law established by the general court. Religious ministers were also paid in the same manner. In Massachusetts Bay, Connecticut, Rhode Island, and New Haven, there are records noting the salary of their governors. Similarly, the salaries of minor officers are referred to in the laws of each colony. At each session, when the salaries of government officials were discussed, records were kept by the recorder. There are also records noting that sometimes governors received only some emolument, but not a salary.

Wages for Governors and Secretaries of State

Governors' wages varied from colony to colony. From 1630 to 1633, there is no evidence indicating that the colonies of Plymouth or Massachusetts Bay had established a law pertaining to the governor's wages. It is pertinent to note that governors in New England did not have a salary for years before the enactment of an act for that purpose. In 1835, Alden Bradford, in his book *History of Massachusetts*, writes that for years, when the colony was small and poor, Governor Winthrop did not receive a salary for his services. Like clergymen, he only received presents, which he later refused to accept. According to Bradford, he refused such presents to avoid being unduly influenced in his official duties. In July 1633, records reveal that members of the Massachusetts General Court reached a consensus on the salary of the governor. In this year, the salary of Governor John Winthrop was £150 per year.[34] In addition, he also received £200 to £300 for his personal money spent for the benefit of the colony.[35] We find a similar law in Massachusetts Bay, which concerned the repeal of the governor's salary. In 1641, during the administration of Governor Richard Bellingham, an order of the general court was passed repealing the law that had established the salary of the governor at one hundred pounds. In 1644, the salary of Governor Endecott was one hundred pounds.[36]

In Connecticut, the general court also passed an order allowing the governor and the deputy governor thirty pounds as their annual salaries. In the same colony, Dwight Loomis notes that the first salary of the governor was regulated in the order of November 9, 1641. According to the order, the salary of the governor was 160 bushels of corn collected from the colony. After four years, the salary was settled to thirty pounds in wheat, peas, and Indian corn.[37] In 1647, the salary of the governor in Connecticut was thirty pounds yearly, as recorded by Loomis. In 1671, the salary for the same government official was £150.[38] In New Haven Colony, the governor and his deputy did not receive a salary for their government work. According to Edward Rodolphus Lambert, Governor Eaton and his deputy governor Goodyear worked for free. It was an honor for them to serve the people and to work toward the general good of the colony.[39]

In addition to the governors' salaries, the salaries of the secretaries of state were also recorded by New England historians. Dwight Loomis writes that Connecticut's secretary of state was paid twenty pounds, including additional fees. Like the secretary, in 1657, the treasurer was paid ten pounds a year for his encouragement. In 1663, he received an increase to twenty pounds yearly.[40]

Minor Officers' Wages

Throughout the New England colonies, minor officers were paid according to the laws established by the general court. In the early years of the various settlements, minor officers were appointed for the execution of laws and other government services. Data from various documents illustrate that magistrates, constables, marshals, prison keepers, surveyors, recorders, and clerks were appointed in many plantations and towns. To illustrate this, in Massachusetts Bay Colony, Increase Nowell was paid forty shillings for his services as a clerk in Charlestown.[41] According to

Richard Frothingham, Jr., Increase Nowell served as secretary of the colony at Massachusetts Bay for many years. He was elected as an assistant of the Massachusetts Bay Company on October 20, 1629, while the office of this company was in England. In addition to the positions listed previously, he was also one of the magistrates in the colony. In Charlestown, he was one of the chief founders, as noted by Frothingham.[42]

In 1637, soldiers were paid one shilling and three pence per day for six days a week of military services. Like soldiers, sergeants were also paid for their work. According to *The Public Records of the Colony of Connecticut*, these military officials were paid each twenty pence per day for the same service. On the other hand, lieutenants were paid twenty shillings per week. In the same period, captains received forty shillings per week.[43] This pay scale reveals to us the payment methods observed during the colonial era. It is worth noting that weekly payment methods date back to the colonial era. In addition to this, the selectmen were chosen by freemen in each town. They were paid twelve pence for their fees for each prisoner under their care, as noted by law. The law also rated the salary of the marshal at twelve pence on the pound. This money was paid to them from the fines, which they collected from various services to which they were entrusted. Moreover, the general marshal was also paid as set forth by the wage's law.

Punishments for Violations of Wage Regulations

Wages were well regulated in the New England colonies. Workers, as well as employers who violated wage regulations, were sanctioned according to the law. Puritan government officials did not tolerate the abuse of wages. In 1673, in Connecticut, excessive wages were considered an oppression. In this case, colonial officials believed that receiving or giving excessive wages was an act of oppressing one's neighbors.[44] William Weeden says that "penalties were prescribed against both the giver and receiver of extra wages. There must be no idleness, under penalty, and special care was devoted to common coasters, and tobacco takers."[45] In 1635, several men were sanctioned for taking excess wages. Those who received two shillings and sixpence per day were punished. According to Weeden, this law was repealed in September of the same year.[46] Despite its repeal, records indicate that in the following years, the general court reinstated this law when it was deemed necessary.

In 1630, the general court fined James Rawlens for taking excessive wages for the work done by one of his servants.[47] According to Joseph Barlow Felt, Rawlens took eight pence for the daily work of his servant. He also had food (meat and drink) for ten days for the same servant, who weeded corn. Upon examination after oath, the court found that Rawlens received the salary of his servant in violation of the law. As a result, he was charged five pence for every day he violated the court order.

The enforcement of wage regulations was also executed in 1630. In the same context of violation of wages, James Loranson, John Callwell, Thomas Danforth, John Gill and his wife, and John Pope appeared at the Court of Assistants for the same infraction.[48] Another case of interest was that of Anker Ainsworth. He was presented to the Court of Assistants for violation of wages.[49] After the court's examination, he was discharged because court officials discovered that he was not in violation of the wage regulations.

In 1639, Edward Palmer was fined for an attempt to defraud the government. According to Edward Hartwell Savage, the author of *A Chronological History of the Boston Watch and Police*, Palmer was employed by the government to build stocks for the punishments of criminals. Upon the completion of the stocks, he presented an exorbitant bill to the general court. As a punishment, he was placed in his own stocks and was charged five pounds for the violation.[50] In 1642, in Connecticut, Thomas Hurlbut was charged forty shillings for exacting [making great demands] and encouraging other people to be paid at a rate above the government order.[51] Based upon these examples, it is clear that Puritan leaders were against exploitation. They did not want citizens or the government to be exploited by people who they believed had evil intent.

Salary of Clergymen

In New England, the accommodations and the salaries of clergymen were ordered by the acts of the general court. In Massachusetts Bay, in 1630, an act was passed for the maintenance of church ministers. In 1642, the general court stipulated that when clergymen were entrusted with government duties, the treasurer of the colony had to defray the charges of the elders of churches for performing special orders of the general court.[52] Massachusetts Bay's laws did not limit their enforcement on the benefits of the clergymen to the service of the government only. In 1654, an order was passed stipulating the responsibility of church members and inhabitants for the accommodation of clergymen. In this year, the court ordered that "the inhabitants of every town shall take care to provide the same, either by hiring some convenient house, for the care of the present minister, or by compounding with him, allowing him a competent and reasonable sum to provide for himself, so long as he should continue with them, or by building or purchasing a home for the minister and his successors in the ministry, as the major part of the said inhabitants shall agree, such assessed upon each person by a just rate, shall be collected and levied as other town rates. There may be a settled and encouraging maintenance of ministry in all towns and congregations within his jurisdiction. Selectmen assess and collect, and levy as other town rates an honorable allowance be made to the ministry."[53] This law was passed in 1654.

Wage Garnishment

Throughout the United States, workers are subjected to wage garnishment by the court. This practice can be traced to the New England colonies. From the *Records of the Court of Assistants of the Colony of the Massachusetts Bay, 1630–1692, Vol. 2*, we discovered that debts were recovered with the enforcement of the court. On November 30, 1630, Sir Richard Saltonstall sued William Knopp for his debt. In this case, the Court of Assistants in Boston decided that William Knopp had to reimburse Sir Saltonstall's money. To enforce this, the court garnished Knopp's wages. As a result, it was ordered that "whosoever employed William Knopp or his son in any work, shall pay the one half of their wages to Sir Richard Saltonstall. Whoever buys boards from them shall pay one half of the price to Sir Saltonstall until the money was paid by them."[54] This is the first recorded case of wage garnishment in colonial New England.

For another example, on March 22, 1631, at the Court of Assistants held in Boston, Richard Johnson was subjected to wage garnishment. He confessed to the court that he owed a debt of thirteen pounds to Sir Richard Saltonstall. After the case was heard, Johnson agreed to pay the sum of money he owned Sir Saltonstall in two weeks' time. As such, the court ordered that those who hired him to work shall pay to Sir Saltonstall eight pence and two shillings per week from his salary.[55] From the case of Johnson, it is easy to discern that the weekly payment that has been observed in the United States was started by the English in the colonies, especially in the colony of Massachusetts.

Chapter 7

Price Regulations in New England

The accounts of price regulations in New England deserve attention in the same magnitude as wages. In the United States, consumers are sometimes misled by advertisers. For that reason, Congress has established laws for the protection of buyers and sellers. Like in the United States, in colonial New England, the prices of goods were regulated according to the laws of each colony. In the same manner, towns were entrusted with the regulation of prices, because it was difficult for the general court to do so. In reading laws enacted in colonial New England, it is worthwhile to assert that the officials regarded the price gouging as immoral, unjust, and evil. In this context, it is normal to note that the colonists' views on pricing were religiously oriented. Similar views are often stated by politicians in the United States with respect to wealth disparities. In a like manner, hospital charges are conceived of as exploitative by many Democrats. Therefore, they often claim that it is immoral to charge high fees for the treatment of poor people or to take advantage of patients without insurance.

Lawmakers in the New England colonies were also religious leaders. They believed that traders who exploited buyers by increasing profits were unacceptable by the law of God. Therefore, they labeled them as evil people. In the same manner, their behavior was categorized as evil. This concept can relate to us that exploitation of poor people was detested by the colonists. For most of the time, New England's colonial officials did not honor such behavior. Even leaders who engaged in such practices were sanctioned according to the established law. Despite the force of law, sometimes mitigating and extenuating factors were taken into account when adjudicating the violations of price regulation laws.

In Plymouth Colony, trade and prices were regulated by orders of the court. On March 29, 1626, the general court prohibited interterritorial trade of corn and beans, due to the scarcity of those products. Accordingly, the court ordered that any person willing to transport corn and beans to different colonies for sale needed a license from the authorities. As punishment for the violation, the court confiscated goods or imposed punishment at the discretion of the governor and the council.[1] In the same colony, in 1632, the general court regulated the price of beer. In this year, the court ordered that the price of beer could not exceed two pence for a Winchester quart.[2] Like beer, wine and strong water were to be sold only in the inns and victualling houses.[3] The keepers were also prohibited from allowing children and servants to buy strong water. The punishment for such violation was five shillings for every infraction. This is the first time we discovered the protection of minors against substance abuse in the colony of Plymouth. Similar laws are observed and enforced in the contemporary United States. Minors are not permitted to purchase liquor or cigarettes, and punishment is reserved for retailers who violate these laws.

The concept of vilifying price gouging was first enforced in Massachusetts. In 1630, price regulations were enforced, but these did not produce a tangible result. According to William B. Weeden, colonists attempted to regulate the prices of goods but failed. His account was collected from the work of Felt. Weeden noted that, when they tried to regulate the trade price at six shillings, the price of commodities rose to ten shillings and twenty shillings.[4] The price increase was due to the scarcity of food in the colony. Charles Brooks, in his *History of the Town of Medford*, elucidated why food was expensive in Medford. He writes that "the anxiety of Medford's first inhabitants must have been very painful. The scarcity of grain [was] great; every bushel of wheat-meal, 14 s. sterling, every bushel of peas, x s. and not easy to be procured either."[5] The information recorded by Brooks clearly reveals why it was difficult to control the prices of commodities in 1630. In 1637, six beads were ordered to be sold at a penny for any sum under twelve pence.[6] According to Weeden, in this statute, only one rate was mentioned.[7]

In 1640, Governor John Winthrop complained about such behavior, also noting that evil practices were present among them. In his journal,

Governor John Winthrop says: "This evil was very notorious among all sorts of people, it being the common rule that most walked by in all their commerce to buy as [they] could, and to sell as dear."[8] According to Alice Morse Earle, in 1634, the general court ordered the price of a meal to be set at sixpence and a quarter of beer at a penny. The price at the Ship Tavern was regulated the same. A person who spent the night at the Ship Tavern paid three shillings per day for fire, bed, food, wine, and beer.[9] Price control was based on the incomes of the inhabitants of the colony. The aim of colonial officials was to protect their fellow citizens against exploitation from traders. In the same token, the colony was poor, and selling commodities at expensive prices was not acceptable at the time. In Boston, town officials were also entrusted with the regulation of prices. Samuel Adams Drake records that "in 1635, the town regulated the price of cattle, and commodities."[10] This town regulation was enacted when New England towns were authorized to make bylaws for the management of their town's affairs.

The price increase was affected when provisions from England arrived in the colony. At the time, money was scarce, so the price of goods depreciated. Governor Winthrop recorded that when a great quantity of provisions arrived in the colony from England and Ireland, products such as cattle and other commodities were sold cheaply. As a result, the general court passed an order for the regulation of prices. The aims of both the governor and the general court were to protect the price of local products. In this case, we can note that the notion of protectionism was observed in the New England colonies. It appears that colonists feared competition against local products, which led them to regulate imported goods. Because the colony was out of money, the general court passed an order declaring that corn shall be used instead of money for payment of new debts. As such, the court regulated the price of Indian corn at four shillings per bushel. Like corn, various local products were also regulated. Rye was set at five shillings, and wheat at six shillings. The order further permitted a resolution between the creditor and the borrower for old debts. In this case, the order of the general court advised the creditor and the borrower to have three witnesses for the appraisal of goods used to pay off debts.

In Connecticut, arbitrary pricing was considered oppression. It is understandable that colonial officials in Connecticut disapproved of the increase of commodities' prices without consideration for the conditions of the people in the colony. During the early years, many settlers were poor and did not have money to afford a luxurious life. Therefore, colonial officials were obligated to protect the poor against the rich. As a result, a law was passed in Connecticut for that end. This law protected workers as well as the prices of goods, and it reads as follows:

> Whereas a great cry of oppression is heard amongst us, and that principally pointed at workmen and traders, which had to regulate without a standard prepared both for advance and for pay duly set as money. It is therefore ordered that the price of provision be duly set at each of General Courts annually, according to true intelligence from Boston, for money sold, and then for such pay within fix money paid, no merchant or trader shall advance above two pence upon the shilling for profit, charge and venture from Boston, or other market of like distance, for goods well bought with ready money; trusting and trifles under a shelling left each man's agreement.[11]

In 1650, in the colony of Connecticut, the court ordered that corn be sold in 1651 at the country rates. In the same year, wheat was sold for four shillings and sixpence per bushel. On the other hand, peas were at three shillings and sixpence per bushel. Rye was sold at three shillings and sixpence per bushel, and Indian corn at three shillings per bushel.[12] Punishments were reserved for the violation of this regulation. According to the *Connecticut Colonial Record*, breaches of this regulation were punished proportionally to the value of the oppression and triple the value of the oppression. As a consequence, one-third of the price was restored to the oppressed party.

Punishments for Violators of Price Regulations

In New England, Puritan leaders and ministers were strict with respect to the execution of laws. According to their religious beliefs, the inhabitants of the colony had to observe God's laws. The Bible was the model that they had to follow. Those who misbehaved were severely punished.

As noted in the beginning of this chapter, the Puritans considered the exploitation of consumers to be an evil act. Therefore, those who dared to do so were punished. According to the price control regulations, no exceptions were reserved for any person whatsoever. To illustrate this, Robert Keayne, a wealthy man, was accused of selling his goods at excessive prices. As a result, a complaint was made against him to the general court. For his misdeeds, he was fined £200 after he was convicted. Due to his moral character, his pain was reduced to one hundred pounds.[13] Again, his moral character was considered. Therefore, his case was moved to the following general court for further examination. After this examination, the court discovered that Keayne had violated price laws many times. For his foreign goods, he was charging his consumers sixpence or more than a shilling over his profit.[14] On April 24, 1657, George Wallis, a citizen of Massachusetts Bay Colony, was charged twenty pounds at the county court for price gouging.[15] Cases brought to the officials pertaining to excessive prices were adjudicated fairly. In 1643, the Stodder case was discharged from the court after he was accused of selling cloth at an excessive price. Upon the investigation of the court, he was found innocent.[16]

Regulations for Markets and Fairs

The history regarding the regulation of markets and fairs in the United States can be traced to the Anglo-Saxon era in England, as well as to the New England colonies. This practice has continued and was perfected by Anglo-Americans. In Massachusetts, from the acts respecting fairs and markets enacted in 1633, data indicate that various towns were permitted by law to establish markets and fairs. For example, the general court authorized local authorities in Boston to have a market on the fifth day of the week from time to time. On the other hand, in Salem, according to the act, they had to open their market on the fourth day of the week from time to time. Like the towns listed previously, in Lynn, the market was open the third day of the week, following the same requirements as Boston and Salem. In Charlestown, the market was operational the sixth day of the week, in accordance with the acts respecting fairs and markets. The town of Boston was allowed two fairs a year on the first third day of the third month. Another fair in this town was held on the first third day of the eighth month for three days each year.[17] The acts regulating fairs and markets were reenacted in 1634, 1636, 1638, and 1648.

In Plymouth Colony, we discovered that, in 1639, the market was regulated by an act of the general court. That year, the court declared, "there shall be a market kept at Plymouth every Thursday, and a fair yearly the last Wednesday in May, to continue many days and a fair at Duxborrow [Duxbury] yearly and to continue two days for all cattle and commodities."[18] Then, in 1643, in New Haven Colony, markets and fairs were regulated by an act of its general court. This act ordered that "there shall be two markets or fairs for cattle and other goods every year at New Haven, on the third Wednesday in May, the other the third Wednesday in September."[19] In Hartford, Connecticut, the court ordered the opening of two fairs each year, one on the second Wednesday of May and the second fair on the second Wednesday of September.[20]

Protection Against Poor and Deceitful Service

Consumer protections in the United States date back to the colonial period. In New Plymouth, the court ordered that, for every bushel not well ground, the miller paid a penalty of sixpence to the client and sixpence to the treasurer for the colony.[21] A similar law was also enforced in the colony of Massachusetts Bay. According to Joseph B. Felt, each miller in Salem and other parts of the colony were ordered by the court to collect no more than one-sixteenth of the corn that they had to grind.[22] In 1635, according to *The Charters and General Laws of the Colony and Province of Massachusetts Bay*, a law was passed for the regulation of millers. Also that year, the court ordered, "no miller shall take above one-sixteenth part of the corn he grinds; and that every miller shall have always ready in his mill weights and scales, provided at his own charge, to weigh corn to and from mill if men desired" (laws of 1635 and 1638).

In 1648, in Massachusetts Bay, the court prohibited shoemakers from refusing to make shoes for any inhabitants at a reasonable price if they provided their own leather. This order covered only people who made shoes for themselves and family members in the New England colonies. During this era, colonial officials required that consumers be treated fairly. Handymen, as well as other businessmen who rendered direct services to the people, were required to serve them as agreed. As an illustration of this, in 1638, the colony of Plymouth regulated the service of millers. In this case, colonial officials prohibited millers at Scituate to take from their customers more than one-sixteenth part of grain for grinding. A penalty was also reserved for millers who did not grind.[23] In 1647, in Connecticut, John Meigs and Henry Gregory were found guilty of deceitful services. Meigs, a shoemaker, sued Gregory for furnishing him poor quality leather and thread. When the case was transferred to the Committee of Shoemakers, both were found to be at fault. Meigs was guilty of encouraging Gregory to use poor materials to make shoes. Gregory and Meigs were found liable for transgressing the rules of righteousness.[24] In our modern era, this can be translated as the violation of trust between consumers and traders. This culture of protecting clients from deceitful or bad services is still used in the United States.

In Massachusetts Bay, many mill owners were punished for deceitful services or for lacking sufficient equipment to operate their mills. In 1639, Willi [William?] Fuller, who owned the mill at Concord, was charged by the court for gross abuse in overtoiling. For this infraction, he was fined three pounds.[25] In the same year, Walham and Richards were also fined five shillings, because they did not have scales and weights in their mills. The court advised them to provide these materials during their next court appearances.[26] By law, each owner of a mill was ordered to have a weight and scales at his mill.[27] This infraction was taken with much consideration throughout the colonies. In Massachusetts, there were mills in many towns. According to William B. Weeden, the first mill in Massachusetts Bay was in Watertown. In 1632 or earlier, Watertown's mill was moved to Boston. With the construction of mills in the colony, a law was enacted for the control of mill owners in Massachusetts. In 1633, Edward Tomlins built a mill in Lynn. According to Weeden, this mill was the second in the colony. In Dorchester, a water mill was also built. Weeden says that it was the first such mill built in the colony.[28]

In Plymouth Colony, by law, any unsealed weights and measures were punishable. The law ordered that wronged parties were awarded restitution by mill owners. Similarly, the owner of a mill who defaulted his clients or used false weights and measures was required to pay the colony treasurer six shillings and eight pence for the first offense. For the second infraction, he paid thirteen shillings and four pence. And for the third infraction, the fine was twenty shillings, and the fraudulent scales were burned by the officials.[29] Honesty in measuring and selling products is also observed by modern Americans. This practice is regulated by laws of the states, as well as federal law.

Transportation Regulations and Pricing

In colonial New England, government officials paid attention to the transportation of people and goods. From the earliest years, records reveal that local ferries and the post office were operational in New England. In towns established near rivers, by the order of the court, some inhabitants opened ferry lines. For example, in Massachusetts Bay, the first towns were built along rivers such as the Charles and Merrimack Rivers. In 1630, the ferry line connected Boston Harbor, Charlestown, and Chelsea. *The Records of the Court of Assistants of the Colony of the Massachusetts Bay, 1630–1692* indicate that the court advised the inhabitants of Boston to apply for a ferry permission for the ferry line between Charlestown and Boston.[30] Like in Massachusetts Bay, in Connecticut, Rhode Island, and New Hampshire, people used the ferry to conduct business and visit family members or friends. Government officials and church ministers employed the ferries for their assigned duties. The *Records of the Court of Assistants*, dated June 14, 1631, note that Edward Converse opened a ferry line between Charlestown and Boston. His ferry fare for each individual person was one pence.[31] In Connecticut, the ferry was operational on the Connecticut River and the Quinnipiac River. Like Massachusetts, Connecticut had many rivers, so ferry lines connected many towns throughout the colony. In Plymouth Colony, at the North River, a ferry line was also operational.

Ferry Regulations

Records show that, in 1630, the ferry transportation from Boston to Charlestown was regulated according to the law set by the authorities. In

1856, Samuel Gardner Drake writes that, in 1630, the ferry from Boston to Charlestown was managed by a ferryman appointed by the governor. They were allowed one penny from every person transported on the ferry and one penny for a hundred pounds weight of goods transported in the same boat. This is the first time that we find evidence for pricing regulation of ferry transportation. In 1636, Thomas Marshall was licensed to keep a ferry from Mylne Point to Charlestown and to Chelsea. He was permitted to transport people and goods from Charlestown to Chelsea for a cost of sixpence for each passenger. For two people, he was also allowed to receive two pence. When the ferry had more than two people, the fare was two pence for each person. Drake notes also water bailies were also appointed for the regulation of waters in towns. In 1638, in New Plymouth colony, the ferryman charged two pence for each person he transported.[32] Jonathan Brewster operated a ferry at North River. He was permitted to carry people who went to plantations. In the first year of his ferry line, the fare for a single person was two pence, and for a horse and his rider it was sixpence. For a beast, the fare was sixpence, and for a swine or a goat, it was two pence for each.[33]

In Windsor, Connecticut, inhabitants used the ferry boat to travel to the river. According to *The Public Records of the Colony of Connecticut*, the ferry fare for a single person was three pence, as ordered by the officials. When the ferryman carried more people in his boat, each person paid two pence.[34] In Norwich, Connecticut, the first ferry was established by Hugh Amos in 1671. His ferry was operational over the Shetucket River.

Regulation for the Protection of the Ferry

According to the *Records of the Governor and Company of the Massachusetts Bay in New England*, in 1641, the general court passed an order setting forth the requirements for people entering the ferry. According to this order,

no person shall press or enter into any ferry boat contrary to the will of the ferrymen, or of the most of the passing upon entered, upon pain of 10 lashes for every such attempt, every ferryman shall permit and allow any person to come into his boat against his will of any of magistrates or deputies or any elders in a boat is 10 pounds. Coming first, or last Physicians, surgeons, midwife, shall be transported as such were first.[35]

In 1641, an act was passed by the general court for the protection of the ferryman from violent people. The law stipulated that the ferryman was authorized to receive his ferry fare before any person entered his boat. He was also ordered to refuse passage to any person who did not pay the fare. The court also ordered that passengers should enter in the ferry according to their arrival time in the line. That means first come, first served. On the other hand, those who came last had to wait until their entrance time arrived.[36]

The Exemption for the Ferry Fee

The law also authorized free passage for magistrates and deputies. These officials were allowed free passage on any ferry in the colony. The same law protecting government officials from having to pay ferry fare was enforced in the province of New Hampshire. According to the *Calendars of State Papers, Colonial Series, America and West Indies*, the ferry law passed by the General Assembly of New Hampshire for the protection of government officials from paying ferry fare declared that

> it is ordered that all that keep ferries within this province shall carry to and fro[m] without any pay all or any of the council, Deputies for the General Assembly, jurymen which are upon the service of the province; and all troopers in their common and general musters shall pay but 3d. horse and man, and foot soldiers only a general muster shall pay one penny a person.[37]

This act was also in force when the colony of New Hampshire was under the jurisdiction of Massachusetts Bay. Thus, in 1641, magistrates and deputies were exempted from paying the ferry fare while working. The act of the general court declared that the officials listed previously were granted free passage on all ferries.[38] In addition to the ferries, the post office was also established in the New England colonies.

The Post Office

The establishment of the post office in New England was first implemented in Massachusetts Bay Colony. According to Samuel Gardner Drake, in 1639, a post office was operational in Boston in the house of Richard Fairbanks. Similar information regarding the post office was recorded in the Collection of the Massachusetts Historical Society. According to this collection, the post office was organized by order of the court. This post was established on September 9, 1639, and the order reads:

> For preventing the miscarriage of letters, it is ordered that notice be given, that Richard Fairbanks his house in Boston is the place appointed for all letters, which are brought from the seas, or sent according to their directions, and he is allowed for every such letter 1d. and must answer all miscarriage through his own neglect in this kind; provided that no man shall be compelled to bring his letter thither except he please.[39]

This order indicates the first post office legislation in colonial New England. Additionally, the title of postman can be traced from this record, with Richard Fairbanks being the first postman in the New England colonies and his house the first post office. Moreover, a mailing fee was also introduced for the first time in New England. The order also reveals that Fairbanks was liable for the loss and destruction of mail. While Fairbanks worked at his house, messengers were the first roving mailmen. But after many complaints of letters getting thrown out or lost, Fairbanks was removed from his position after Boston merchants filed a petition to the Massachusetts General Court to remedy the situation.[40]

In January 1673, messengers were officially accredited as roving mailmen who deserved wages. According to the general court records of this year, an order was passed for this purpose. The order of the general court reads:

> whereas the public occasions of the country do frequently require that messengers be sent post and as yet no stated allowance is settled in such case it is ordered by this court and the

authority thereof that from henceforth every person so sent
upon the public service of the country shall be allowed by the
Treasury after rate of 3d. a mile to the place to which he is sent,
in money, as full satisfaction for the expense of horse and man.
And no inholder shall take of any such messenger or other traveling upon public service more than 2s. per bushall [bushel] for
ootes and 4d. for hay, at day and night.[41]

This was the first order of the court of Massachusetts setting a rate for
the payment of any person engaged as a traveling postman in the public
service.

CHAPTER 8

Regulations of Schools and Trainings
in New England

Educational instruction in New England was just as important as the planting of the colonies. The concept of building schools in the colonies was set forth in charters authorizing Englishmen to settle in New England. As a result, colonists brought with them books and teachers for that purpose. With respect to instruction, among the founding fathers of the New England colonies, there were Cambridge graduates. As such, they were men who valued education as well as progress. In addition to Cambridge, colonists attended Oxford University and other colleges either in England or Scotland. It is no wonder that in Massachusetts, Harvard University was established with the same ambitions as Cambridge University in England. Like Harvard, grammar schools were modeled after those in England. As university graduates, it is sound to speculate that there were many educated immigrants in New England who attended to the domestic education or grammar schools in their home countries. Such educated people were often employed as teachers in grammar schools in their respective towns or plantations. In Massachusetts, colonists established dame schools, elementary schools, secondary schools, and colleges.[1] In the seventeenth century, private schools were also instituted in various towns.

Before the discussion of the educational institutions in New England, it is better to briefly explore the emergence of schools in England. The history of education there can be traced back to the tribal era. From the work of Caesar, data indicate that youth in Britain were instructed by the Druids.[2] Parents sent their children to the Druid learning institutions to be instructed in their religion. According to Caesar, the Druids did not commit their religion in writing. Roman writers such as Julius Caesar and Tacitus recognized the talent of the Druids in astronomy, mathematics, and physics. From this account, we can speculate that through their religion, Druids priests institutionalized their education to some extent. Upon the invasion of the Romans, tribesmen in England witnessed a different type of instruction. In this case, they were taught Latin and Greek.

In the year 78 after the birth of Christ, during the reign of Julius Agricola, the Romans' school of education was introduced. According to Nicholas Carlisle, Agricola instituted the Roman arts and sciences. He also encouraged the children of British nobles to learn Latin and the Roman culture. Carlisle notes that Roman teachers were entrusted with the education of noble youth of Britain.[3] Many English also had access to an education in Rome. When the kingdom was later Christianized, many schools were opened in monasteries by bishops and cardinals. Nicholas Carlisle writes that, in monastic and Episcopal schools in England and in other European countries, the youth were instructed to read and write Latin and to sing and play church music to prepare them for the public offices of the church.[4]

Arthur Francis Leach writes that in the medieval era, during the time of Bede, a grammar school was established in East Anglia in 631.[5] Like Leach, Thomas Wright, in his book *Anglo-Saxon Period* writes that a school was established in East Anglia before 635 during the reign of Sigebert or Sigbertch.[6] The Venerable Bede writes that Sigbertch, the king of East Anglia, was baptized in France during his exile. Upon being Christianized, he was instructed in that country. When he returned to Britain, he established a school for youth in an imitation of those in France. The aim of establishing a school in his kingdom was to educate the youth in literature. As a visionary king, he invited Bishop Felix, a Burgundian, to help with that mission. Felix furnished masters and teachers from Kent. In addition to a school, King Sigebert also built a monastery.[7] The work of A.D. Bayne indicates that Bishop Felix established his bishopric at Dunwich, which was also the capital city.[8] Accordingly, Sigebert also resided at this capital. Due to the importance of the city, it is likely that the school built by the order of King Sigebert was established there. During the reign of Sigebert, Felix built many churches and monasteries in East Anglia. He also converted the inhabitants of Suffolk and Norfolk to Christianity.

Because monasteries were often connected with schools, they were also established in other parts of the kingdom. At Burgh, Saint Fursa or Fursey, with the support of King Sigebert, built a monastery that was named Cnobheresburg, after the Saxon chief of that town, who lived there.[9] In London, Saint Paul's School has also been around since antiquity. During the reign of King Henry I, Hugh was appointed the schoolmaster [headmaster] of that institution.[10]

In Shrewsbury, there was also an established school as early as 1080.[11] This school was noted by Ordericus Vitalis, who studied in Shrewsbury when he was five years old. Vitalis, an Anglo-Norman, entered the school in Shrewsbury to learn grammar. In the same town, on October 10, 1232, King Henry I appointed Roger of Abboteslee as schoolmaster.[12] Like Leach, Nicholas Carlisle recorded that few schools were established during the medieval era. In his work *A Concise Description of the Endowed Grammar Schools in England and Wales*, he writes that during the reign of King Richard II, a free grammar school was established at Wisbech. He believed this school was originally founded by the Fraternity or Guild of the Holy Trinity in 1379.[13] Another school that deserves notice is the free grammar school at Penrich, founded in 1395 during the reign of King Henry II.[14] In Saint Mary of Ottery, John Grandison, the Bishop of Exeter, purchased a manor and church of Ottery with the aim of founding a school. In 1337, a noble college was established in Ottery Parish Church.[15]

Historically, New England colonists observed educational principals and methods that had been utilized in England. From various documents written by English writers, records revealed that their domestic schools, grammar schools, and colleges or universities were legally recognized academic institutions. Educated people were entrusted with their management and organization. To illustrate this, Roger Ascham, an educated Englishman, was entrusted with the education of young boys, as well as noblemen.[16] In the colonies, like in England, evidence shows that educated people were also charged with the teaching of young boys. Similarly, in New England, the same procedure was observed and enforced. In addition to teaching and establishment of schools, we find also that regulatory laws were enacted to manage these academic institutions. Records show that New England schools were likewise subjected to regulations from their towns, counties, and colonies. We also discovered that training or apprenticeship was utilized as one of the methods to instruct scholars in both England and the colonies.

From records of various documents, authors indicate that New England inhabitants emigrated from eastern and western England from the counties of Essex, Dorset, Devon, Lincoln, and Dorchester. In these counties, records revealed that grammar schools were established during the reigns of rulers such as King John, Henry I, Henry II, Henry VI, Henry VII, Henry VIII, Queen Mary, and Queen Elizabeth. Grammar schools were founded under the letters patents ordered by the crowns of England. Some schools were established when the inhabitants and local officials petitioned the kings for that purpose. Sometimes, schools were built with money accommodated by the wills of honorable people who believed in the education of youth. These same methods were observed in the New England colonies. In Massachusetts, for example, a Charlestown minister named John Harvard left money in his will for the establishment of a college in the Massachusetts Bay Colony.[17] Meanwhile, in Connecticut, Edward Hopkins left money for the establishment of a grammar school for the youth of Hartford and Hadley. In addition to money left in wills, there were also donations collected from colonists and government officials.[18] Like grammar schools, home tutoring was also observed, like in England. Pertaining to regulations, some grammar schools were made corporations and bodies politic by the kings' letters patents. This was the case of the grammar school established in 1551 at Sherborne in Dorset County, which was made a "Body Corporate."[19] As such, after the school's foundation, a body of statutes was enacted for its administration. The same procedure was adopted in Massachusetts Bay when Harvard College was established. Much about the college in Cambridge will be discussed later in this chapter.

In England, the methods of educating youth varied during different times. At first, domestic education and trainings were observed throughout the kingdom. In the same context, grammar schools were institutionalized also as training for apprentices. For those who finished grammar school, the door to college or university was open. The same system was also observed in New England. Grammar schools were founded to prepare students for college or university. On the other hand, learning a trade was used to help them enter the work market, so they could be useful for the commonwealth.

Training Concepts

It is true that the charters issued to the New England colonists ordered the building of schools, but there is no evidence that there were any colleges in the colony before the establishment of Harvard. But from the first letter written to Governor Endecott in New England, we discover that the training of servants was critical for the development of the colony. According to the views of the Massachusetts Bay Company, skilled servants were important to train young people in the skills needed for the future of the colony. For example, the company ordered the instruction of two or more youths by Lambert Wilson, a chirurgeon (surgeon), when he came to New England.[20] Wilson made an agreement with the company to serve for three years on the plantations, and his duty was to treat patients in the plantations. In addition to the English, Native Americans also received medical care from Wilson, as noted by the company.[21] The officials of the company believed that those trained young people would replace Wilson in the plantations. The leaders of the Massachusetts Bay Company in England advised Governor Endecott to select first the son of Higginson, the pastor of Salem, for training under Wilson, because he was trained in literature, although what literature he was trained in was not specified.[22]

In the second letter, the company also stressed the training of youth. At this time, they desired servants to be under the tutelage of Richard Claydon, a wheelwright. According to this letter, Claydon was an honorable person and was recommended to them by Dr. Wells. Accordingly, they wanted him to train many servants as wheelwrights.[23] This order of the leaders of the Massachusetts Bay Company is the first evidence we have stressing the priority of training the youth in the plantations. The same concept was also advocated by government officials in the New England colonies. The term "apprentice" was commonly applied in the colony, with their instruction being almost the same as that in our modern vocational schools.

From *The Charters and General Laws of the Colony and Province of Massachusetts Bay*, we discovered that government officials encouraged the training of youth into different trades. According to an act of the general court, youth who were incapable of attending school or learning were ordered to learn a trade to better their lives and to be useful for the commonwealth. In May 1642, the general court ordered that "all parents and masters do breed and bring up their children and apprentices in some honest lawful calling, labor or employment, either in husbandry, or some other trade, profitable for themselves, and the commonwealth, if they will not or cannot train them up in learning, to fit them for higher employment."[24] It is certain that a law was passed by local officials in Boston requiring boys and girls be taught to spin flax in 1642. In this town, those who made the best linen, after being spun and woven, received money from the town as a sign of encouragement.[25] Like in Boston, the spinning of flax was regulated by law in other villages in Massachusetts. According to the information collected by James Otis from the account of Ruth of Boston, lawmakers of nearby villages ordered that every family shall spin so many pounds of flax each year or pay a very large amount of money for not obeying the law.[26]

This law explicitly reveals how the colonists observed educational systems set forth by their forefathers, the British. In England, kings employed university graduates for the administration of the kingdom's affairs. We discovered many university graduates in the kings' cabinets in England, such as Rev. Wolsey and Anthony Bacon. In New England, a similar approach was also put into effect. As noted in previous chapters, there were many university graduates in Massachusetts Bay, Connecticut, and Rhode Island. The Anglo-Americans also reserved higher positions for highly educated people. Likely, they encouraged their countrymen to engage in lawful and gainful employment. On March 28, 1637, in Connecticut, the court ordered Francis Stiles to train George Chapple, Thomas Cooper, and Thomas Barber in carpentry while they were his servants.

Military Training

Military training was regulated by laws enacted by the general court in each of the New England colonies. New England colonists came from

a country with a long history of warfare. Tribal men in the island of
Albion fought each other consistently, but conflicts also originated from
outside the nation. Foreigners like the Romans and Germanic tribes
attacked the island and occupied it for their own profit. Due to these
military attacks, men in England were always training in the art of war.

During the reign of King Alfred, the national militia system was introduced. In this case, all male subjects in the entire kingdom became militiamen.[27] Like King Alfred, King Henry II also valued militia training.
According to Captain A. E. Lawson Lowe, King Henry II reestablished
the annual training of the militia. He termed this training the "Assize of
Arms."[28] Contrary to King Alfred, King Edward I specified the ages of
persons qualified for militia duties. The Statute of Winchester of 1285,
which was enacted during his reign, stipulated that "all freemen between
the ages of fifteen and sixty were bound to serve in the Fyrd (or militia),
but only in their respective counties, except in case of invasion."[29] This act
was also observed in the New England colonies. From many documents,
we discovered that the laws ordered healthy men between the ages of fifteen and sixty to perform militia duties. In 1612, King James I introduced
the trained band system in England.[30] This force was entrusted to the
military jurisdiction of each county's lord lieutenant.

Like their forefathers, New England officials instituted the same
policy. Every male in the colonies was trained in the field of war. They
received training from experienced and skilled military men. In Massachusetts, military instruction was established in 1630. For this purpose, each town paid a tax for the salary of a military instructor. Charles
Brooks writes that the inhabitants of Medford paid three pounds for
this purpose. Men enlisted in military training received knowledge in
military tactics so they could become trained soldiers.[31] On July 6, 1631,
the General Court of Massachusetts "ordered that every first Friday
in every month, there shall be a general training of them that inhabit
Charlestown, Mystick, and the Newtown, at a convenient place about
the Indian Wigwams; the training to begin at one of the clock in the
afternoon."[32] In this law, data reveal that military training in the New
England colonies was structured. Cadets were informed about the place
and time where they were to be trained. Likewise, inhabitants selected
for the training were mentioned in the law.

In 1635, the formation of military men into companies was func-
tional in Massachusetts Bay Colony. Brooks tells us that the inhabitants
of Medford, Cambridge, and Charlestown formed one company in 1635.
On November 20, 1637, the general court "ordered that training should
be kept eight times in a year, at the discretion of the chief officers." This
law exempted magistrates and teaching elders from this training. Like
the magistrates and church elders, the deacons of several churches bene-
fited from the same exemption.[33]

After many military companies were formed in Massachusetts Bay,
a law was passed to manage them. On September 7, 1643, the general
court noted: "it is agreed that the military commanders shall take order
that the companies be trained, and some men, to be appointed by them,
in each town, to exercise them."[34] Like adults, children were also trained
in military skills and tactics. On May 14, 1645, the General Court of
Massachusetts Bay

> ordered that all children within this jurisdiction, from ten to
> sixteen of age, shall be instructed by some of the officers of the
> band, or some other experienced soldier, whom the chief officer
> should appoint upon the usual training-days, in the exercise of
> arms, as small guns, half-pikes, bows and arrows, according to
> the description of said officer.[35]

This law specified the types of arms with which cadets were trained. In
the same way, the method of selecting military training for youth was
noted. Moreover, the ages of cadets ordered for military service were
also specified.

In Connecticut, like in Massachusetts, the same approach was observed. The training of military men was placed under the jurisdiction
of the best selected officers. In 1636, according to *The Public Records of the
Colony of Connecticut*, the commissioners or lawmakers ordered military
training in the colony. The order of this year stipulated that inhabitants
of every plantation schedule military training once a month. If they did
not have a skilled military trainer, the plantation was permitted to appoint one. In the same order, a skilled military officer was mandated to
inspect weapons to determine if they were serviceable.[36] In 1637, Captain

Mason was appointed as a public military officer of the colony. In that capacity, he was assigned with the training of military men in each plantation following his scheduled day and time. His annual salary was forty pounds, which was to be paid out of the treasury.[37] For better communication with military men, the law ordered him to announce his training days two weeks in advance.[38]

Regarding the same aspect of training in Connecticut, Isaac William Stuart writes that in the trained band, the tallest soldiers were trained as pikemen, and those of lower stature received training as musketeers. Furthermore, the officers of a trained band were well instructed in the field of war. According to Isaac William Stuart, officers of a trained band were requested to know martial duties, to behave courageously and wisely, to be temperate, "to have a fatherly care" over their soldiers, "to teach them how to fight upon all occasions," and if in battle, "to lead them up first against the enemy."[39] This illustration by Stuart informs us how military commanders were trained and expected to behave on the battlefields of New England. In a like manner, it reveals the fatherly culture of modern military officers toward the men in their battalions or companies. In Connecticut, Captain Mason was appointed chief of the training band. Training was not the only approach employed for the education of inhabitants of New England. Domestic schooling was also prevalent in the early years of the colonies.

Domestic Education

The history of domestic education can be traced back to England, where the colonists came from. This system is from antiquity and was observed for many generations, even when grammar schools were introduced in the kingdom. Records from many books reveal that princes and children of noblemen were often under the care of learned men for that purpose. To illustrate this, Sir Simon Burley was the tutor of King Richard. At the request of Edward the Black Prince, Burley was given the responsibility of tutoring Richard while he was a child. From this tutoring, Richard and Burley became friends.[40] King Edward was under the tutelage of John Cheke. According to John Strype, Cheke was a religious guide and teacher to King Edward when he was a youth.[41] Similarly,

Queen Elizabeth received an elementary education with the assistance of her tutor, Roger Ascham.[42] In the kingdom of England, Ascham has been credited for instructing many people of note on how to write and read. Charles John Smith notes that Charles, Duke of Suffolk; Prince Edward; and Lady Jane Grey were other students of Ascham.[43]

Another case that fits this context is that of Robert Cecil, the son of Lord William Burleigh. Due to his deformation, he was instructed at home under the care of a tutor before entering Saint John's College, Cambridge, in 1550.[44] Many educated young Englishmen grew up to serve the king. John Strype recorded that trained youth or scholars were employed for the service of the king and court, to be ambassadors, secretaries, privy counselors, bishops, and tutors to the nobility.

There is no evidence indicating that formal schools were established in Plymouth or Massachusetts Bay prior to the foundation of Harvard College. The accounts of various local New England authors, however, indicate that domestic schooling was observed throughout the colonies. Charles Brooks, a local historian in Medford, Massachusetts, wrote about pertinent data on domestic schooling in that city. According to Brooks, domestic instruction was the only method utilized by the colonists before the institutionalization of formal education.[45] For example, Roger Williams was a domestic teacher in Rhode Island. According to Thomas B. Stockwell, in 1654, "Roger Williams taught two young gentlemen by words, phrases, and constant talk."[46] In this case, he was a scholar and a teacher. Alice Morse Earle, in her *Customs and Fashions in Old New England*, stresses that Puritans more heavily emphasized religious teaching. According to her, education in New England had many religious features.[47] The Bible and Bay Psalm Book were the first reading materials for students in New England. The catechism was one of the methods of religious instruction for youth.

Like Earle, Charles Brooks asserts that the Bible and primer were the reading books used for teaching. He also notes that in plantations and towns where the clergymen were paid, the teaching of youth was the responsibility of such ministers. According to him, it was customary for boys to reside with the minister's family for college preparations.[48] In this case, ministers were pleased to educate youth, whom they received in their family home. As educated people, ministers were qualified for such duties.

It is essential to note that in the early years of the colonies, the inhabitants of many plantations and towns were poor. Thus, they could neither afford to establish a school nor to pay a minister for the education of their children. In such places, youth were sent to the neighboring towns to receive an education. This was the case of Medford in Middlesex County, Massachusetts.[49] To some extent, ministers volunteered for such duties. Domestic education also served as a preparation for grammar schools for those who mastered writing and reading. In the same context of domestic schools, dame schools were instituted in Massachusetts Bay.

Dame Schools

In New England, neither economic prosperity nor population density was parallel throughout the colonies. Some towns were highly populated, whereas others did not have more than fifty inhabitants. Therefore, the Act of 1647, which ordered the establishment of grammar schools in towns or plantations inhabited by fifty to one hundred people, was not feasible in towns and plantations with less than fifty residents. As a result, dame or domestic schools became more common.

In addition to the financial prosperity, in towns where teachers utilized rigid rules, parents tended to send their daughters to dame schools. Accounts of the establishment of dame schools in Massachusetts have been noted by many writers, such as Harlan Updegraff, author of *The Origin of the Moving School in Massachusetts.* Like Updegraff, Charles H. Walcott, in his book *Concord in the Colonial Period: Being a History of the Town of Concord, Massachusetts, 1635–1689*, recorded pertinent information about the existence of dame schools in that town. In addition to the previously mentioned authors, James Otis wrote a book titled *Ruth of Boston: A Story of the Massachusetts Bay Colony*. Otis writes authoritatively about the establishment of a dame school in Boston. His book was pieced together from the recollections of an English immigrant in Boston as well as those of a student at the Boston Grammar School, including the dame school. From these accounts, Otis informs us that Ruth of Boston attended a dame school in Boston. From her recollection, Ruth noted that the dame schools were taught by women.[50]

In Boston, this approach was established due to the rigid rules employed by Master Philemon Purmont at the grammar school. According to Ruth, tenderhearted people perceived the methods employed by Purmont as too harsh for younger children. As a result, after one year of his work in that school, Mistress Sowerby was hired as a teacher at the dame school for a yearly salary of six pounds. Her job description was to teach the girls and smaller boys.[51] At the dame schools, students were also trained in various professional fields, such as spinning tow strings and knitting hose or stockings. Moreover, students learned how to cook, weave, and knit, because the school was located at her house. She also taught students how to quill.[52] In Concord, Charles H. Walcott notes that John Smedly and Thomas Dakin reported the existence of a dame school in that city. In their report, Smedly and Dakin note that in 1680, in every quarter of Concord, men and women taught children how to read and write English when their parents could spare them.[53]

In addition to Boston, dame schools were instituted in various towns throughout Massachusetts. Arthur C. Boyden, the principal of the State Normal School in Bridgewater, recorded that, in 1673, there were dame schools in Woburn and Hornbook.[54] In Woburn, Updegraff writes that the wives of Allen Convar and Joseph Wright were dame school teachers. In Billerica, the general court reported that there were several dame schools for the instruction of young children.[55] The model used in Boston and Woburn was also observed in Braintree. According to Updegraff, Margery Hoar, the wife of Braintree's teacher and pastor of the church, was the dame of the early time. He went on to note that she had young children in her school from Braintree and other towns, but especially from Boston.[56]

Elementary Schools

In Massachusetts, elementary education started with the enactment of the 1642 law. This same year, the court discovered that parents and masters neglected the education of their children. Likewise, children were not trained for employment. As a result, the selectmen of each town or plantation were entrusted with monitoring and enforcing the elementary education of reading and writing. Parents or masters who neglected the instruction of their children were subject to punishment. The law required that children be able to read and understand the principles of religion and the capital law of the country. Additionally, children who were not able to work were placed in apprenticeships by the court or the magistrate.[57] For better understanding, masters in the colony of New England had servants whom they brought with them from England. Others employed servants while they were in the colony.

From the *Charters and General Laws of the Colony of Massachusetts Bay*, records show that masters and families were instructed to catechize their children once a week at the very least. This was the first law enacted in Massachusetts regarding the instruction of elementary education in the colony. In this year, local officials in Dedham opened an elementary school by providing land for the support of the schoolmaster through an act. According to Henry Suzzallo, Dedham officials did not elect a teacher for the school.[58] Arthur C. Boyden, the principal of State Norman School in Bridgewater, records that 1642 was the instauration of free schools in Massachusetts. According to his perception, the system of universal schooling instituted in Massachusetts was enforced by the selectmen. This education was given in homes. He went on to note that a school was built in Dedham and was supported by public taxation.[59] This account of Principal Boyden corroborates that recounted in *Ruth of Boston*. Accordingly, we discover that children were educated at home before they entered grammar school.

According to Ruth's account, "her mother and father taught her lessons at home. And when Master Purmont opened the grammar school in Boston, she was able to write fairly."[60] Home instruction, which Ruth received, is one of the indications that parents did obey the law. It is difficult to ascertain how many children were educated at home before entering grammar school. Understandably, we do not have data indicating the number of children who were able to write and read from home instruction. Even though children received writing instruction at home, it seems that that education was not sufficient for some of them. Ruth says that the "first lesson in the use of a quill came from him [Master Purmont], I had never known how to form a letter, because of this being exceeding harsh in his ways."[61] She went on to note that "a child who failed in doing at the first attempt exactly as Master Purmont thought, was given a sharp blow over the knuckles of the hand which held the quill."[62] Ruth gives an example of a student who was severely punished for failing to write as Master Purmont requested. She named Ezra Whitman as a victim of the writing instruction of Master Purmont. According to her, "[Ezra] Whitman was punished in this manner so severely on a certain day."[63]

Grammar Schools

The history of grammar schools is critical for our understanding of the modern educational system. This type of school was the equivalent of modern high schools. Students who graduated from grammar school were qualified to attend colleges or universities. In New England, schools were established by the orders of general courts and town meetings. In 1635, records show that formal education was introduced in the colony of Massachusetts. With the contribution of Rev. John Cotton, a grammar school was established in Boston, Massachusetts. According to historians, the Boston school followed the model of Boston, England, where Rev. Cotton served as vicar.

In April 1635, Philemon Purmont was appointed schoolmaster in Boston, where his duties were teaching and nurturing children.[64] At the time when Master Purmont was entrusted with the instruction of young boys, the school was placed at the house of Josiah Plastow or Plaistow of Boston, which was, at that moment, the property of the town of Boston.[65] Otis's *Ruth of Boston* described the setting of the classroom. According to Ruth's recollections, "the classroom had benches set up around the four sides, in such fashion that the scholars faced a ledge of puncheon planks, which was built against the walls to be used when we needed a desk on which to write, or to work out sums in arithmetic."[66] She went on to say that, Master Pormont [Purmont] sat upon a platform in the center of the room, where he could keep us children well in view, and woe betide the one who neglected his task.[67]

Plaistow, or Plastow, moved to Plymouth after being convicted by the Court of Assistants in 1631. He was charged with a misdemeanor, and the court declared that people call him Josiah instead of Mr. Josiah.

Possibly due to this humiliation, he was forced to settle in Plymouth Colony. In colonial Massachusetts, the title "Mr." was an honorific qualification. According to Joseph B. Felt, the author of *Annals of Salem, from Its First Settlement*,

> The title of Mr. was applied to captains and sometimes to mates of vessels; to military captains; to eminent merchants; to schoolmasters; doctors; magistrates; and clergymen; to a person, who has received a second degree at college, and who had been made freemen. The wives and daughters of those men, who were called Mr. were named Mrs.[68]

It seems clear that Plaistow felt that he was denigrated when the Court of Assistants reduced his status to that of a lower-class inhabitant of the colony.

In 1641, authorities in Boston ordered the improvement of Deer Island for the maintenance of a free school. The inspection of the school was entrusted to the selectmen, or townsmen. One of the duties of the selectmen was to make sure that the school was well equipped. This order indicates the values local officials had regarding town schools. Like Deer Island, in 1649, Long Island was also placed under similar conditions. On this island, the selectmen were authorized to lease an acre for a year at sixpence. The money collected was then used for the school.[69] In 1636, Daniel Maude was also selected as schoolmaster of the free school. This school was supported by volunteer donors such as Gov. Henry Vance, who contributed ten pounds. Both John Winthrop and Richard Bellingham served as governors in Massachusetts and donated thirty pounds. In addition to these government officials, forty-two private people also donated, sometimes thirty pounds or four shillings, according to their financial abilities, for the same purpose.[70]

In 1639, in Dorchester and Roxbury, Latin schools were established following the Boston model. Oliver Ayer Robert, the author of *History of the Military Company of the Massachusetts, Now Called The Ancient and Honorable Artillery*, notes that John Bowles was the founder of a grammar school in Roxbury. Bowles was a member of the general court in 1645.[71] From the work of Francis S. Drake, we discovered that Isaac

Heath was the principal founder of the grammar school in Roxbury. Drake also noted that Isaac Heath left a will in which he charged John Bowles with the maintenance of the school that he had founded. Like Bowles, Isaac Heath was a member of the general court from Roxbury.[72] It seems that Heath had confidence in the moral character of Bowles because he was a ruling elder of the church in that city. Historically, Bowles was one of the pioneers of the Massachusetts Bay Company's colonizing movement in New England.[73] Like the officials listed previously, John Eliot, the Indian Apostle, was also the principal promoter of the grammar school in Roxbury. As we noted the promotors of the school, it is also pertinent to discuss one of the original donors to the school. According to the transactions of the Colonial Society of Massachusetts, Daniel Denison was one of the principal donors of the Latin school in Roxbury.[74] Various historical documents revealed that, in 1645, sixty-four inhabitants of Roxbury consented to erect a free school. The maintenance of the free school was also under their care. In this year, the feoffees were empowered with the management of the school.[75] There were seven in total, and the salary of the schoolmaster was decided by them. In Roxbury, they authorized the schoolmaster to be paid twenty pounds per year. The salary of the schoolmaster was collected from the townspeople according to their financial abilities. Each person was required to donate an amount of money ranging from 1.4 shillings to two shillings a year.[76]

With the establishment of a grammar school in Roxbury, Daniel Welde was appointed its teacher. Drake writes that he was the first teacher ever appointed in Roxbury. In 1652, Welde was ordered to provide good benches with forms, tables for students, and a seat for the schoolmaster. In addition to the previously listed items, he had to secure a desk where the dictionary was placed and shelves for books.[77] In 1654, Welde was entrusted with recording births and deaths in the same town.[78] In 1680, Thomas Barnard, a Harvard graduate, was employed as teacher in Roxbury. He was one of the students who had received education at the grammar school in Hadley, Massachusetts. He taught at the Roxbury school for two years after his college studies. At Harvard, he had studied theology.[79] In regard to the quality of the Roxbury Latin School, we discovered that John Wise, a native of that city, went to Harvard College after finishing his education at the Roxbury Latin School. At Harvard, he had also studied theology and was ordained as pastor of the church at Ipswich in 1683.[80] Another native of Roxbury who became a teacher after studying at Harvard was Joseph Hawley. He was employed as a teacher at a school in Northampton, Massachusetts, in 1677. In addition to his teaching duties, he was a surveyor and legislator.[81] Inhabitants of Roxbury were advocates for the establishment of schools in that town. One of these school pioneers was Thomas Bell, who left land and various properties for the support of a free school in 1671. As a result of the school advocacy, many families in the town of Roxbury had many scholars who had attended Harvard College and public schools.[82]

Like Roxbury, Salem officials also ordered the establishment of schools. In 1637, John Fisk, who was a teacher in Newton, came to Salem as the assistant of Hugh Peters as a minister. With that position, he was also entrusted with the instruction of scholars for three years.[83] In 1640, Edward Norris was entrusted with the instruction of the grammar school.[84] In 1644, school-age children were recorded by order of the court. Parents were ordered to prove if they were able to pay school fees for their children. Children from poor families were placed under the care of the town. In this case, taxpayers were responsible for the education of poor children.[85] In this year, according to Charles M. Endecott, Governor Endecott was the first government official to advocate for the free school system.[86] In 1670, town officials in Salem employed Daniel Epes as a teacher. In the same year, Edward Norris was still a teacher in Salem. It was in 1672 that town officials decided to build a school for scholars. As a result of this decision, the old meetinghouse was demolished so that materials from it could be used to build the schoolhouse. In 1673, a committee was appointed for the erection of the school building, which also served as a watchhouse and town house.[87]

In 1639, records indicate that a school was maintained in Dorchester. In this year, the Dorchester Antiquarian and Historical Society writes that "Thompson's Island was disposed for the use of the town school."[88] At Thompson Island, in 1668, the town regulated the thousands of acres reserved for the school. In this year, the town declared that the land given for the school could never be utilized for any other purpose, nor could even a part of it be sold, but it must be reserved only for the use of the free school.[89] Thomas Waterhouse taught a school in that town. In Dorchester, local officials valued properties reserved for the use of schools. In 1668, "it was voted that the thousand acres given to the use of the school should never be alienated to any other use, nor sold, any part of it, but be reserved for the maintenance of a free school in Dorchester forever."[90] In Dorchester, Good Samaritans also contributed financially for the support of schools. For example, one of the Dorchester settlers, named Gibson, gave a pasture for the school to use.[91]

John J. Currier notes that Anthony Somerby seems to be the first schoolteacher employed in Newbury for the instruction of young boys.[92] Due to his teaching work, in 1639, he received four acres of the upland over the great river. In addition to his teaching work, he also served as a town clerk in Newbury. The school in this town was placed at the new meetinghouse built upon in the upland by Abraham Toppman. It was on October 5, 1675, that the town voted at the meeting of the freemen for the establishment of a grammar school.[93] On November 10, 1675, a grammar school was established in Newbury according to the laws of the colony. In this year, Henry Short was selected as schoolmaster in Newbury. His salary was five pounds for the first half of the year and was paid out of the town rate. He also received sixpence from every scholar (student) who attended his school.[94]

In 1647, the Massachusetts General Court ordered the construction of free schools in each town in the colony. It is pertinent to note that the education law of 1647 was the first of that kind, ordering the establishment of public schools in the United States.[95] The acts respecting schools brought to light the educational system instituted in the colony of Massachusetts Bay. In this act, the general court stressed the importance of elementary, secondary, and college education. The law of 1647 ordered each town composed of fifty families to appoint a teacher for the writing and reading instruction of children.[96] These teachers were paid by the parents or masters of the children, or the public of the town. This is the first time we found in colonial America that school was locally regulated. In addition to the salary of the teacher, the 1647 act prohibited the financial exploitation of those who sent their children to elementary schools. It is likely that, after children mastered writing and reading, they were sent to grammar school. The law also gave the selectmen regulatory power for the management of schools. Selectmen felt that it was imperative that decisions about how the schools function remain with them, at the local level.

Like in towns with at least fifty families, the law stipulated that, in towns of a hundred families or householders, the inhabitants had to establish a grammar school.[97] For the administration of the school, a qualified and competent schoolmaster had to be appointed. Like the grammar school, there was an upper level of education, and the requirements for the employment of a schoolmaster were also demanding. One of the requirements was that the schoolmaster prepare students for studying at the university level.[98] This requirement tells us how the notion of having the best teachers at the best schools in America was valued during the colonial period. The same philosophy and approach have been observed in America. In the United States, the notion of hiring the best teachers is important for the reputation of the school, the town, the state, and the country. To avoid making the law useless, an enforcement mechanism was included in the act. As a result, any town that did not establish a grammar school was sanctioned according to the law. As stipulated in the acts respecting schools, a yearly fine of five pounds was collected from towns that violated the act. In addition to instruction, the Massachusetts General Court explicitly emphasized the preparation of youth for real life after school. The law stipulated that for the welfare of this country, its youth must be educated not only in good literature but also in sound doctrine.[99] This clause clearly explains the importance colonialists placed on training students for being productive in their endeavors. Like in towns of fifty families, sanctions were also reserved for failing to establish a grammar school in any town composed of a hundred houses. The fine for such violations was ten pounds per year as prescribed by law. The fine was paid to the next town that established a grammar school in accordance with the act of May 1671.[100] In 1683, an additional clause was added to the Act of 1647. In this year, the court ordered that any town inhabited by more than five hundred people had to establish two grammar schools and two writing schools.[101] Any town violating this law had to pay twenty pounds to the general court.[102]

In Dedham, Massachusetts, in 1644, a portion of land was reserved
for the support of the school. In 1651, the inhabitants of the city decided
in the general meeting that the salary of the schoolmaster was twenty
pounds for a period of seven years.[103] It was also ordered in the same
meeting that the school fees for children ages four to fourteen years was
five pounds per year, which had to be paid by their parents. Money paid
by parents served for the salary of the schoolmaster.[104] From the account
of Henry Suzzallo, we discovered that in 1642, inhabitants of Dedham
planned for the establishment of a school by providing land for the support of a schoolmaster.[105] In 1671, Benjamin Thompson was employed by
the selectmen of Charlestown as a teacher. His employment description
and benefits were as follows:

> 1. He shall be paid thirty pounds per annum by the town, and to
> receive twenty shillings a year from each scholar that he taught,
> to be paid by those who sent children to his school. 2. He shall
> prepare such youth to be capable of going to college. 3. He shall
> teach children how to read, write, and cypher. 4. Any charge or
> remove of either party was to be regulated after a warning was
> given.[106]

The town school in Charlestown was established in 1636. According
to George Leroy Jackson, in this year, William Withrell was ordered to
keep a school for the period of twelve months. It was also settled that he
would be paid forty pounds for his work for the entire year. In 1679, after
the school was neglected, Samuel Phips was appointed as its teacher. On
March 10, 1679, it was voted at the town meeting that a schoolmaster
be appointed to teach children Latin, writing, cypher, and reading English. In 1636, in Braintree, the order of the court declared that parents
educate their children and give them work training and employment.
Failure to obey the order of the court was punishable by paying a fine
after the judgment of the grand jury. According to Samuel A. Bates, the
fines were charged to the selectmen who did not enforce the order.[107] In
the same order of 1636, another provision authorized two magistrates
to place disruptive or delinquent children in apprenticeships if their
parents did not give them a proper education. Regarding the school,

records show that in 1648, Dr. John Morley bought a schoolhouse from Henry Flint with the condition that the school would be recuperated by Flint if Dr. Morley left Braintree. In Braintree, Henry Flint was always called teacher. Like Flint, Dr. Morley taught a school in Braintree for a short period of time. In 1679, Benjamin Thompson was appointed as the schoolmaster in Braintree. His salary was thirty pounds, and he was also given a piece of land to build a home.[108]

In Weymouth, Massachusetts, the Weymouth Historical Society recorded pertinent data on the existence of a school for the education of children. The Society notes that the account recording schools in Weymouth can be traced back to March 10, 1651, when the town voted that Captain Perkins be paid ten pounds for the duration of six months for his service as schoolteacher.[109] In the same document, we discovered that on September 18, 1678, the town was ordered to furnish a schoolroom. In 1680, James Stewart sold his house to the town for the use of the schoolmaster. In 1681, a schoolhouse was erected in Weymouth on a portion of land that had been purchased from Captain John Holbrook. After the school was built, the remaining land was used to build a meetinghouse.[110]

In Cambridge, at Harvard College, a grammar school was also instituted. Lucius R. Paige, author of *The History of Cambridge, Massachusetts*, notes that a grammar school for the instruction of young scholars was established at Harvard College. Young people who entered that grammar school were prepared for college entrance. They were accepted at Harvard College when grammar school officials determined that they were ready for collegiate studies. Paige notes that Elijah Corlet was appointed as schoolmaster for Harvard College's grammar school. There, Corlet taught English and Indian children. According to Paige, in 1643, Corlet was reputed as a schoolmaster with good skills and who was faithful to his profession, until his death on February 25, 1686 or 1687.[111] The grammar school at Harvard College was also noted by Francis Jackson, author of *History of the Early Settlement of Newton, County of Middlesex, Massachusetts from 1639 to 1800*. Jackson writes: "By the side of the college is a fair grammar school, for training up young scholars, and fitting them for academic learning, and as they are judged ripe, they may be received into the college."[112] Jackson collected this information from an observer who, in 1643, mentioned the existence of grammar school at the Cambridge college in his work.[113] In 1642, local officials in Cambridge entrusted selectmen with the management of schools. In that year, town officials ordered the town be split into six parts or divisions. As such, each selectman was responsible for a division, with the aim of determining if all the children received an education according to the law of 1642.[114]

In the colony of Plymouth, children's education was just as valued as religious teaching. In Taunton, John Bishop was listed as the schoolmaster. According to Samuel Hopkins Emery, the school in Taunton was in the same building as the meetinghouse. In 1636, in Plymouth, Mrs. Fuller was ordered to keep children in school for the duration of two years.[115] As the town became populated, in 1663, the General Court of Plymouth Colony ordered the erection of schools in various towns. In 1677, free schools were established in Plymouth Colony. According to Emery, the general law of Plymouth ordered the establishment of grammar schools in larger towns. In 1670, the right to fish from Cape Cod was granted to towns that established a free school, clerical school, and elementary school. In 1682, the General Court of Plymouth divided money generated from the fishing at the Cape as follows: twelve pounds for the Barnstable school, eight pounds for the Duxburrow school, five pounds for the Rehoboth school, three pounds for the Taunton school, and two pounds was given to Mr. Daniel Smith.[116] In 1668, in Hingham, the selectmen of that town recorded the existence of a school in the First Book.[117] In 1670, Henry Smith agreed with the selectmen to teach children until the end of the year. He was entrusted with the teaching of Latin, Greek, English, writing, and arithmetic in Hingham. He was paid twenty pounds quarterly, the value of wheat, rye, barley, peas, and Indian corn. In 1673, James Bates received a salary from the town for keeping a school. In 1674, Joseph Andrews and James Bates were teachers in Hingham and received salaries as schoolmasters. In 1677, a contract was signed between James Bates and the selectmen for his schoolwork. He agreed to teach Latin, English, writing, and arithmetic for twenty pounds a year.[118]

In New Haven, Connecticut, in 1636, an order of the general court empowered each town to establish a grammar school. In this colony, records show that Ezekiel Cheever was the schoolmaster and was paid twenty pounds a year. In 1644, his salary was thirty pounds per year. Due to a misunderstanding between him and the church, Cheever moved to Ipswich.[119] The teaching of Cheever was credited by one of his students. The famous and best-selling poet Michael Wigglesworth, one of his students, noted that in 1639 he studied at the house of Cheever, where he taught pupils. Edward Elias Atwater notes that Wigglesworth received a good education under Cheever, the schoolmaster.[120] In 1643, Andrew Adams was a schoolteacher in Hartford. His annual salary was twelve pounds, as noted by Royal Ralph Hinman. In addition to Adams, William Andrews was a schoolmaster in Hartford. Hinman tells us that Andrews was an early settler in Hartford and resided in the first land division in 1639. The contract he signed with the selectmen for his duties as schoolmaster was sixteen pounds in 1640, as well as in 1643. As was the custom at the time, like in Massachusetts, a grammar school was also established in Connecticut.

In 1650, the schoolmaster in New Haven was paid by the town. In addition to Cheever, in 1651, Edward Elias Atwater discovered that William Jeanes taught school in New Haven for a short period of time. He was paid ten pounds for his teaching work. In October of the same year, Jeanes informed New Haven officials that he had been offered a better teaching position in Wethersfield. This account provides clear evidence that a school also existed in Wethersfield. In Guilford, Rev. John Higginson was also a schoolmaster, in addition to his duties as an elder of the church. At the time when he was a schoolmaster, the salary of Rev. Higginson was paid by the treasurer of the town. Similarly, in 1656, Jeremiah Peck, a minister, was also a schoolmaster in Guilford. His duties as a teacher ended in 1660, when he became a schoolmaster, as established under the auspices of the colony. In 1660, a law was passed that ordered all children to be taught how to read.

In Hartford, Connecticut, Alfred Andrews writes that William Andrews was a schoolmaster in 1639. In addition to these duties, he also served as town clerk. In 1640, William was a teacher in Hartford, and his salary was thirty pounds.[121] In 1672, the county school system was introduced by law in Connecticut. As a result, Hartford had, for the first time in the history of the colony, a countywide free school. This school was supported by donations from various people, such as John Talcott, in 1649. Following Talcott was the donation from William Gibbins in 1654. Like Talcott and Gibbins, in his will, Edward Hopkins left land and properties for the support of schools in the colony.[122]

In 1640, in the colony of Rhode Island, a measure was taken to establish a school for poor students. By a vote of colonial officials, one hundred acres of land was set aside for that purpose. In this town, poor students were encouraged to receive formal education.[123] The account of the Newport school was noted by Richard M. Bayles, the editor of *History of Newport County, Rhode Island*. He writes that, in 1640, the town of Newport employed Robert Lenthal to keep a public school for the instruction of youth from poor families. For the building of the school, four acres of land for a house lot were provided by the town, in addition to two hundred acres of land for his services as a teacher. Moreover, one hundred acres was reserved for the support of the school.[124] Town officials permitted him to sell or lease land reserved for the support of the school. With respect to Lenthal, Thomas Williams Bicknell notes that he was a clergyman. He was made a freeman before his employment as teacher. According to Bicknell, Lenthal taught school in Newport until 1642, when he left for England.[125] He went on to state that Lenthal's arrival to Newport from Massachusetts Bay was intended to replace John Clarke.[126] With respect to the establishment of the school, Bicknell mentioned that John Clarke and Coddington were the original promotors of education in Newport. The school in Newport was free of charge for everyone's children. It is sound to note that this was the first time in the New England colonies such an approach was put into execution. In Massachusetts Bay, parents were, from time to time, charged with the support of the schoolmasters according to their financial abilities.

In 1663, the General Assembly granted a hundred acres of upland and six acres of meadow to the town of Providence for the maintenance of a school. It seems that this is a palpable example indicating the existence of an established educational system in Providence. Ten years later, a school was also established in Barrington, at the time when this city was part of Swansea, Massachusetts.[127] Like other towns in Rhode Island, in 1680, land was granted for the use of the schoolmaster in Bristol.

According to Thomas B. Stockwell, this is the first record pertaining to the construction of a school in Bristol, which was opened in 1682.[128]

Private Schools

The institutionalization of school in the United States dates back to the colonial period in Massachusetts Bay. It is a concept that had been passed down from the English to the Americans. In the book titled *A Handbook of American Private School: An Annual Survey*, we discovered that private schools existed in the colonies from the beginning of the settlement. In this document, the dame school was listed as a private school. Similarly, schools established by ministers were also identified this way.[129] According to Arthur C. Boyden, private schools began in 1673 and continued to be in use from this date. He mentioned that in the town of Hornbook, there existed a private school.[130] Tuition was required to attend this private school. In Andover, private schools were operated by the wives of ministers. Sarah Loring Bailey, the author of *Historical Sketches of Andover (Comprising the Present Towns of North Andover and Andover), Massachusetts*, writes that Mr. Woodbridge and Mr. Dane, ministers, kept a private school. This private school in Andover was more likely a prominent school because it was associated with Benjamin Woodbridge. According to Bailey, Woodbridge was one of the first Harvard College graduates, and he settled in Andover.[131] As a graduate of a reputed academic institution, the school run by his wife more than likely held high standards. Many prominent people also lived in Andover, such as Bradstreet. Therefore, private schools were established for these upper-class families. Rollo La Verne Lyman, the author of *English Grammar in American Schools before 1850*, records that in Connecticut, private schools of a lower grade existed during the colonial period. According to his data collection, some private schools were kept in Hartford and Windsor. He notes that Goody Betts kept a dame school in Windsor until 1647, when she died. In her school, Betts taught young children by using the hornbook.[132] In the same document, Lyman revealed that Rebecca Parker established a school in Malden, Massachusetts for a long period. In Salem, Widow Catherine Dealland was paid fifteen pounds for her teaching services.

School Committees

In New England, behavior and institutions were controlled through regulations set by government officials. Throughout the history of New England colonists, we discovered that rule of law was an instrument of change. To illustrate this, when magistrates were deciding cases according to their own discretion or will, the inhabitants requested that the law be codified for the better governance of the colony. Like in the judiciary, the court entrusted selectmen with the administration of schools, to avoid the same corruption. From the work of Henry Suzzallo, we discovered that the selectmen were empowered with the hiring of teachers, support, or providing a location for the building of a school.[133] In addition to the selectmen, the elders of the church were also included in the administration or management of schools. Therefore, the selectmen, elders, and superintendents of schools formed the school committee. With the formation of this body, school supervision was regulated according to the laws enacted by each town. In colonial New England, schools were under the jurisdiction of towns or plantations.

Officials appointed for the supervision of schools differed from town to town. In 1644, records indicate that wardens were appointed in the city of Dorchester for the management of the school. The duties of the warden were the monitoring of the schoolmaster and students. In this year, Howard, Dea Wiswell, and Atherton were appointed for life as wardens in Dorchester. They were moved from that office upon committing a serious offense. Dorchester Antiquarian and Historical Society believes that the school wardens can be called the first school committee. In Newbury, John J. Currier, author of *Newbury, Massachusetts*, writes that on November 29, 1652, Mr. Woodman, Richard Kent Jr., Lieutenant Pike, and Nicholas Noyes were appointed to school committees for the management of the business of the schools.[134]

College

The concept of establishing upper-level education was not conducted in isolation. Colonists in New England, especially in Massachusetts, regulated the colony following Anglo-Saxons' norms in England. With their acquaintance with Cambridge University and Oxford University, they decided to open a college of such magnitude for their children and other dignitaries in the colony. Along with their own children, poor scholars and Natives Americans could also have access to the same institution. It is pertinent to note that colonists in Massachusetts had the same vision as Cambridge University regarding the training of religious ministers. Additionally, they wanted to prepare quality young people to carry on their legacies. In Connecticut, such ambition was also prevalent among religious and government leaders. For example, in 1654, Rev. Davenport proposed to the general court the establishment of a college in New Haven Colony. As a result, the town donated a portion of land for that purpose.[135] But his vision was materialized in the 1700s with the foundation of Yale College.

Harvard College

The history of the American colleges can be traced to the colony of Massachusetts, where, in 1636, the general court passed a law for the building of a college in the colony. On September 8, 1636, the general court in Massachusetts Bay passed an act ordering the establishment of a college in Massachusetts. In 1638, the general court decided the cost for the construction of Harvard College was £400. The £400 was to be paid in two installments. In 1639, the general court passed an order instructing that the college be built at Newtown (now Cambridge). In addition to the money provided by the general court, Rev. John Harvard, a philanthropist, declared in his will that one-half of his estate be used to build Harvard College. As a result, the school was named after him.

Overseers of the College and the College Corporation

In 1642, for better management of the college, the general court assigned government officials with the power of regulating that institution. As a result, the governor, deputy governor, and all the magistrates in Massachusetts were overseers of Harvard College. In addition to the government officials named previously, teaching elders from the towns of Cambridge, Watertown, Charlestown, Boston, Roxbury, and

Dorchester, including the president of the college, were also empowered with the same duties.[136] According to the court, "[they] have full power and authority to make and establish all such orders, statutes, and constitutions as they shall see necessary for the instituting, guiding and furthering of the said college and the several members."[137] This was the first time in the history of the colony that government officials were associated with the administration of a college.

In 1650, Harvard College became a corporation and a body politic organization. With this juridical power, a body of qualified officials was entrusted with the management of the college. According to the Massachusetts Bay Company records, a president, five fellows, and a treasurer or bursar were the governing officials of Harvard College. In this year, records indicate that Henry Dunster was the first president of Harvard College. Among the five fellows were Samuel Mather, Samuel Danford, Jonathan Mitchell, Comfort Starr, and Samuel Eaton. Thomas Danford was treasurer for the college. These Harvard officials were all inhabitants of the Massachusetts Bay Colony.[138]

Financial Assistance for Poor Students

Financial assistance is an essential ingredient that renders college education affordable for all Americans. It is also a source of income for colleges and universities. It is sound to note that without recourse to financial aid, many Americans would have difficulty attending colleges and universities. Because of this, New England colonists observed the same norms as in England in helping poor students. Financial aid was a settled culture among the English. In England, money was collected from private sources and from guilds or societies for the support of poor students. Like in England, in the New England colonies, government officials and private donors were encouraged to support poor college students at Harvard College. This action was operational in the Massachusetts, Connecticut, and New Haven colonies.

To better regulate donations received for poor students at Harvard College, in 1641, the General Court of Massachusetts enacted a law regarding benevolence and charitable donations. The act respecting benevolence or charitable donations ordered that "all gifts and legacies given and bequeathed to the college, and schools of learning or any other public use, shall be truly and faithfully disposed of according to the true and declared intent of the donors."[139] This act was implemented to avoid abuses of the donations collected for legitimate use. Like in Massachusetts, the New Haven court selected two people for the collection of school or public use donations, and this proposition was approved in 1644. On November 11, 1644, the court ordered that Joshua Attwater and William Davis receive a peck of wheat or its equivalent from volunteers in the plantations for the support of poor students at Harvard College.[140] It appears that these were the only persons entrusted by law as collectors of money or its equivalent for the education of poor students.

In 1652, the court made an important order pertaining to the support of poor students. This act can be termed financial aid as in our modern era. In this year, the court ordered a volunteer collection of money from the inhabitants of the colony for the support of the president and poor scholars at Harvard College. To raise additional funds, an honorable person from each town in the colony undertook the volunteer work for collecting money. The order also permitted the secretary of state to communicate with the governors of other colonies to encourage their citizens to do the same. This order also requested voluntary assistance from other colonies for the same purpose. The court appreciated the collections made by volunteers, which were for good purpose.[141] The order of this court is pertinent because it educates us that financial assistance for poor college students is a historical act in the United States. It is pertinent to note that the establishment of Harvard College was a historical act for the colonies. Therefore, donations were collected from various towns in the New England colonies. To illustrate, in 1653, the town of Concord bequeathed five pounds a year for seven years for management of Harvard College. When the officials erected Harvard Hall in 1672, the inhabitants of Concord agreed to pay forty-five pounds as a donation for that purpose.[142] In addition to financial assistance, Rev. Peter Bulkley donated a portion of his books to Harvard College's library. According to Paige, he had a large personal library at the time when he bequeathed part of it to the college.[143] Like other towns in Massachusetts Bay, in 1669, a general collection was proposed in New Hampshire for the support of Harvard College and for the building of a new edifice.

In this year, Portsmouth agreed to contribute sixty pounds annually for the period of seven years. On the other hand, the town of Dover gave thirty-two pounds and Exeter ten pounds.[144]

On May 3, 1654, the court limited access to the school environment to moral people only. In this year, the court ordered that the overseers of the college and the selectmen in various towns restrict immoral or scandalous people from entering the school premises or being allowed to instruct students. People who were not in conformance with the rules of Christ were also prevented from being near the college or entering into the schoolyard. The overseers of Harvard College and the selectmen of various towns in Massachusetts assumed the same duties that the college police or private security officers do at college campuses. Due to death or other conditions, overseers of Harvard College were, from time to time, updated. In 1654, John Allin, a pastor in Dedham; John Norton, a teacher at Boston; and Thomas Cobbett, a pastor and teacher at Lynn, were added to the list of Harvard College overseers.

Colonial officials in Massachusetts Bay understood the value of education. Having matriculated from prestigious universities such as Cambridge and Oxford, they desired to put Harvard in the same ranks as their alma maters. To accomplish this, they lamented how the president and fellows of the college were not well supported. According to them, God was grateful in guiding them through their journey to New England. He also helped them in instituting a college that was useful to the church and the commonwealth. Most likely, the school was useful to other New England colonies. They feared neglecting the college was an ungrateful act to their posterity and to God. Therefore, they ordered that ten pounds be withdrawn from the colony treasurer for the salary of the president and fellows. This amount of money was to be distributed to the school officials in accordance with the will of the overseers of Harvard College. On October 23, 1657, an order was passed by the court for the management of Harvard College. An appendix to the college charter stipulated that "it is ordered the corporation shall have power from time to time to make such orders and bylaws of the college, as they see cause."[145] In addition to the management of Harvard College and the salary of the president, the college was also empowered with its jurisdiction.

Judicial Jurisdiction of Harvard College

It is important to briefly explore the history of the judiciary jurisdiction of Harvard College. From the various documents consulted, records show that Harvard College was the first institution of higher education established in New England. There were no precedents revealing how the behavior of students should be regulated in a college in the New England colonies. In Massachusetts, the behavior of students at Harvard College was regulated according to the court's order. This law is the first in the colonies indicating that the school was empowered to regulate the students' conduct in the same manner as the local court did. On October 4, 1656, the president and fellows of Harvard College were entrusted with minor judiciary duties for the regulation of students. According to the law, the president and fellows in their discretion had the right to punish all misdemeanors committed by students. In this institution, students were punished by paying a fine or being whipped in a public setting according to the nature of the offense. Regarding the fine, the court authorized the college to charge students less than ten shillings. In the case that a whipping was required, ten stripes were allowed for one offense. Accordingly, the court ordered the continuation of this law until the overseers of the college presented a different approach to punish students.[146] It is sound to note that even in our modern era, colleges are entrusted with minor judiciary jurisdiction.

Chapter 9

Summary and Conclusion

*P*ilgrims and Puritans in Colonial America: Regulatory Laws in the *New England Colonies, 1630–1686,* gives an account of the regulatory laws promulgated in the New England colonies by the general courts for the organization of schools, price control, military training, employment, and wage control. In addition, this book recounts the duties of lawmakers and the methods utilized for the promulgation of these many laws. Examples of these include examinations of colonial laws such as the Massachusetts Body of Liberties, the Connecticut Code of 1650, and the Rhode Island code law of 1663. Furthermore, this work investigates the demographic history of the founders of the New England colonies like John Winthrop, John Cotton, Roger Williams, Rev. John White, Roger Ludlow, Thomas Hooker, John Haynes, Rev. John Davenport, and Theophilus Eaton. The data regarding the founders of New England is significant because it correlates with the laws they enacted for the regulation of the economy, religions, courts, employment, and schools.

Moreover, data pertaining to New England colonists reveal pertinent information on their governing styles, as well as the maintenance of law and order. In this book, the academic institutions that the colonists attended in England and Scotland are attentively examined. Historically, many New England colonists were alumni from Cambridge and Oxford. With those academic degrees, they established civilized colonies in accordance with Christian values they acquired from universities in England. This largely shared culture has been subsequently observed by Anglo-Americans.

As noted previously, the book also discusses the discovery missions conducted by English subjects in North America. The work of explorers such as Captain John Smith, Sebastian Cabot, and his children is pieced together. In a like manner, the impacts made by English explorers such as Sir Francis Drake, Sir John Hawkins, and Plymouth and Bristol merchants are noted. This work also points out the contributions made by the crowns of England for the completion of discovery missions in the same region. The impacts made by King Henry VII, King Henry VIII, Queen Elizabeth, King Edward VI, King James I, and King Charles I were investigated. Equally, the formation of the Plymouth Company and the Council for New England, which served as catalysts for the founding of the New England colonies, are analyzed. Similarly, the incorporation of the same organizations is elucidated. The Council of New England was a body that had the legal power to sell land to the architects of the planting of colonies in New England.

The movement enacted by the colonists in Massachusetts Bay and New Plymouth for Connecticut is thoroughly explained, as is the planting of colonies in Rhode Island by the inhabitants banished from Massachusetts Bay. The foundation of New Haven Colony by Rev. John Davenport and Theophilus Eaton is briefly explored. The migrations of inhabitants of Massachusetts Bay and Connecticut inhabitants to Long Island are discussed.

Finally, school regulations in the New England colonies are saliently examined. The establishment of domestic, dame, elementary, grammar, and private schools is detailed in this work. The schools in the colonies followed the same model as the English schools. The contributions of monks and religious leaders in the building of schools in England are stated. Additionally, the book explores the history of Harvard University, pointing out the duties of the overseers of the college, the corporation of the institution, and the assistance of poor scholars. Moreover, the judiciary jurisdiction of Harvard College is briefly detailed.

Endnotes

Introduction

1. William B. Weeden, *Economic and Social History of New England, 1628-1789* (Boston: Houghton, Mifflin, and Company, 1890), 79–81. In this book, Weeden discussed regulations regarding wages in colonial Boston and Dorchester. In both towns, Weeden also noted regulatory laws enacted for the admission of strangers. According to him, in 1636 strangers were not welcome in Boston for more than fourteen days without the permission of town officers. In Dorchester, a similar law was enacted in 1658, stipulating that inhabitants of that city were not allowed to shelter a stranger without the consent of the selectmen.

2. See Nathaniel Bouton, *Provincial Papers. Documents and Records Relating to the Province of New Hampshire, from the Earliest Period of Its Settlement* (AMS Press, 1868), 64, 100, 119, 129, 156–57, and 290–91.

3. See *The Collection of the Massachusetts Historical Society* (Boston, Charles C. Little and James Brown, 1838), 48–60.

4. John Winthrop, *The History of New England from 1630–1649, Volume 2* (Phelps and Fornham, 1826), 4, 7, 18, 22, 24, and 55.

5. See *Bulletin of the United States Bureau of Labor Statistic, No. 6004, History of Wages in the United States from Colonial Time to 1928, Vol. 523* (Washington, DC: United States Government Printing Office, 1934), 1–5.

6. Ethelbert Stewart, "Bricklayers Wages and Conditions: Colonial to Organization Days," *The Bricklayer, Mason and Plasterer* xviii, no. 12 (1915): 273.

Chapter 1

1. Edward M. Hartwell, Edward W. McGlenen, and Edward O. Skelton, *Boston and Its Story, 1630-1915* (City of Boston Printing Department), 1916, 7.

2. John Josselyn, *Account of Two Voyages to New England, made during the Year 1638, 1663* (London: Giles Middowes, 1674), 229.

3. Francis Bacon, *Bacon's History of the Reign of King Henry VII* (Cambridge: University Press, 1885), 171–72.

4. Richard Johnson, *A New History of England. From the Earliest Period to the Present Time. On a File Recommended by the Earl of Chesterfield, etc.* (London: E. Newbery, 1775), 89.

5. Henry Duff Trail, *Social England: From the Accession of Edward I to the Death of Henry VII* (New York : Putnam, 1894), 495.

6. Adam Anderson, *Anderson's Historical and Chronological Deduction of Origin of Commerce, from the Earliest Account . . . Carefully Revised, Corrected, and Continued to the Year, 1789, by Mr. Coombe, Vol. 2* (Dublin: P. Byrne, 1790), 9–10.

7. Ibid.

8. Ibid., 14.

9. Ibid.

10. Trail, *Social England: From the Accession of Henry I to the Death of Henry VII* (New York: Putnam, 1894), 489–90.

11. Ibid., 494.

12. Ibid., 16.

13. Ibid.

14. Anderson, 27.

15. John Josselyn, *Account of Two Voyages to New-England* (London: Giles Widdowes, 1674), 229.

16. Anderson, 10.

17. Francesco Tarducci, *John and Sebastian Cabot* (Detroit: H. F. Brownson, 1893), 124.

18. Ibid., 117–18.

19. David Hume, *The History of the Reign of Henry the Eighth: Written by David Hume, Vol. 2* (London: D. Brewman, 1792), 12.

20. Ibid.

21. Giles Jacob, *Lex Mercatoria: Or, the Merchant's Companion, Containing All the Laws and Statutes Relating to Merchandise* (London: Publisher not identified, 1718), 16.

22. Archibald. Allardice, *Lives of the Most Eminent British Naval Heroe* (Leith: Printed by and for Archibald Allardic, 1809), 2.

23. Henry Richard Fox Bourne, *English Merchants: Memoirs in Illustration of the Progress of British Commerce, Vol. 1* (London: R. Bentley, 1866), 152.

24. Ibid., 198.

25. Ibid., 197.

26. Richard Johnson, *A New History of England. From the Earliest Period to the Present Time. On a File Recommended by the Earl of Chesterfield, etc.* (London: E. Newbery, 1775), 91–3.

27. James Fawckner Nicholls, *The Remarkable Life, Adventure and Discoveries of Sebastian Cabot, of Bristol: The Founder of Great Britain's Marine Power, Discoverer of America, and Its First Colonizer* (London: S. Low. Son, and Marston, 1869), 151–53.

28. Ibid.

29. Ibid., 157.

30. Patrick Colquhon, *Treatise on the Wealth, Power and Resources of the British Empire in Every Quarter of the World Etc.* (London: Joseph. Mawman, 1814), 1.

31. See William Camden, *Annals, or, the Historie of the Most Renowned and Victorious Princess Elizabeth, Late Queen of England*, trans. R.N. Gent (London: Printed by Thomas Harper, 1635), 42.

32. Ibid.

33. Ibid.

34. Ibid., 86.

35. Ibid., 91 and 219–20.

36. William Robertson, *The History of Discovery, and Settlement of America* (New York: Harper & Brothers, 1831), 395.

37. See *Calendar of State Papers: America and West Indies, 1574* (Great Britain. Public Record Office. Longman, 1860), xi.

38. Lucy Aikin, *Memoirs of the Court of King Charles the First, Vol. 1* (London: Longman, Rees, Orme, Brown, Green, and Longman, 1833), 30.

39. Ibid.

40. Ibid.

41. Robertson, 403.

42. See *Calendar of State Papers*, 20.

43. Ibid., 25.

44. *Calendar of State Papers*, 5.

45. Ibid., 5. Data in the *State Papers* show that on April 10, King James granted to Sir Thos Gates, Sir Geo Somers, Rich. Hakluyt, Prebendary of Westminster, Edward. Maria Wingfield, Thos Hamon, Raleigh Gilbert, Wm. Parker, Geo-Popham, and divers others, of Virginia . . . to be divided into two several colonies.

46. Jacob Bailey Moore, *Lives of the Governors of New Plymouth, and Massachusetts Bay* (New York: Gates & Stedman, 1848), 9.

47. See *Calendar of State Papers*, 24.

48. Ibid., 96.

Chapter 2

1. William Robertson, *The History of Discovery, and Settlement of America* (New York: Harper & Brothers, 1831), 401.

2. Josselyn, 243. The voyage of Captain Bartholomew Gosnold was completed under the reign of King James. He traveled from Falmouth in a small bark accompanied by thirty-two men.

3. George Bancroft, *History of the United States of America, from the Discovery of the Continent [to 1789], Vol.1* (Boston: Little, Brown, and company, 1876), 90–1.

4. Alexander Brown, *The First Republic in America* (Boston and New York: Houghton, Mifflin and Company, 1898), 8.

5. Ibid., 5.

6. Ibid.

7. William Hunt, *Bristol* (London: Longmans, Green, 1887), 40.

8. See Richard Nicholls Worth, *The History of Plymouth from the Earliest Period to the Present Time* (Plymouth: W. Brendon and Son, 1873), 58.

9. Josselyn, 244.

10. William Hubbard, *A General History of New England: From the Discovery to MDCLXXX* (Boston: Charles C. Little and James Brown, 1848), 72.

11. Patent of incorporation; see *Calendar of State Papers, Colonial Series* (Great Britain: Public Record Office, 1860), 24.

12. Ibid., 88.

13. Ibid., 96.

14. Ibid., 97.

15. Ibid.

Chapter 3

1. Walter Moore, *Boston (Lincolnshire) and Its Surroundings: with an Account of The Pilgrim Fathers of New England* (London: Homeland Association, 1908), 32. Sir Robert Naunton explained to the king that the Pilgrims' colonization was intended to enlarge the Gospel by all due means. As King James I believed in the propagation of the Gospel, he approved their plans. The King said to Sir Naunton that his response regarding the enlargement of the Gospel was a good and honest motion.

2. Joseph Barlow Felt, *The Annals of Salem: From Its First Settlement* (Salem: W & S.B. Ives, 1827), 47. Felt says that "Lady Arabella Johnson was daughter to the Earl of Lincoln, whose family was highly esteemed, and deeply interested in the welfare of New England."

3. "The John Winthrop Papers," in *Collections of the Massachusetts Historical Society, Vol. VI,* Fourth Series (Boston: Printed for the Society, 1863), 1.

4. *Record of the Company of the Massachusetts Bay in New England, Vol. 1* (Cambridge: Bolles and Houghton, 1850), xix.

5. Ibid., xix.

6. See *The Chronicles of America Series: Pilgrims and Puritans* (New Haven: Yale University Press, 1919), 3.

7. Ibid., 23–24.

8. See *Records of the Colony of the Massachusetts Bay in New England* (Cambridge: Bolles and Houghton, 1850), xxiii.

9. John Brown, *The Pilgrim Fathers of New England, and Their Puritan Successors* (New York: Fleming H. Revell Company, 1895), 243.

10. Ibid.

11. Felt, 5.

12. See Dorchester Antiquarian and Historical Society, *History of the Town of Dorchester, Massachusetts* (Boston: E. Clapp Jr., 1859), 14.

13. See William Paterson, *The Merchant Princes of England* (London: London Society, vol. 7, 1865), 450.

14. Ibid.

15. Thomas Hutchinson, *The History of . . . Massachusetts Bay* (London: M. Richardson, 1765), 9.

16. R. N. Worth, *The Plymouth Company. See Report & Transactions, vol. 14* (Plymouth: Devonshire Association for the Advancement of Science, Literature and Art, 1882), 3, 59.

17. Henry R. Stiles, *The History of Ancient Windsor, Connecticut, including East Windsor, South Windsor, and Ellington, Prior to 1768* (New York: Charles B. Norton, 1859), 6.

18. Brown, 273.

19. Quote from the letter of King James I to his western counties' lieutenants; *see Calendar of State Papers,* xxi.

20. Ibid.

21. Weeden, 13.

22. John Camden Hotten, *The Original Lists of Persons of Quality, Emigrants, Religious Exiles, Political Rebels, Serving Men Sold for a Term of Years, Apprentices,*

Children Stolen, Maiden Press, and Other who Went from Great Britain to the American Plantations, 1600–1700 (London: Chatto and Windus, 1874), xvii.

23. Ibid., xxii.

24. Frederic Calvin Norton, "Biographies of the Governors of Connecticut," *The Connecticut Magazine*, vol. 7, 1901, 59.

25. Brown, 266.

26. Ibid., 267. Brown says that "Suffolk in the Southern portion of Eastern England made an important contribution of the Puritanism of America when it sent John Winthrop from Groton Manor-house. Lincolnshire made the most important contribution Bostontown, or Sempringham."

27. George Ripley and Charles A. Dana, *The New American Cyclopaedia: A Popular Dictionary of General Knowledge, Vol. 3* (New York: Appleton, 1867), 613.

28. Charles Brooks, *History of the Town of Medford, Middlesex County, Massachusetts: From Its First Settlement, in 1630, to the Present Time, 1855* (Boston: James M. Usher, 1855), 34.

29. See John Stevens and Saint Bede the Venerable, *The Ecclesiastical History of the English Nation* (London: T. Meighan, 1723), 41–44. Bede notes that Vortigern invited the Saxon Nation. He noted that nation of Angles or Saxons arrived with three ships and had a place to reside assigned to them by the king in the eastern part of the island.

30. Ibid., 46.

31. Wilhelm Zimmermann, *A Popular History of Germany: From the Earliest to the Present Day, Vol. 1* (New York: Henry. J. Johnson, 1878), 169.

32. Ibid., 170.

33. See Bayard Taylor, *A History of Germany from the Early Times to the Present Day* (New York: D. Appleton, 1894), 200–300. Taylor says that "the Cherusci, the Chauci, and other tribes named by Tacitus, were incorporated with the Saxons, who exhibited the same characteristics."

34. John Whitaker, *The History of Manchester in Four Books, Vol. 2* (Manchester: Newton, Clark, and Harrop, 1775), 19–20. Whitaker writes that "the Jutes lived on the Southern Shore of Scandinavia." He also indicated that this tribe emigrated from Scandinavia to Germany. They settled in the Cimbric Peninsula and in the territory of the Cimbri. He described them as being a piratical nation.

35. Zimmermann, 242–43.

36. Whitaker, 20.

37. Ibid., 13.

38. Wright, 5–13, 23, 40, 95.

39. George William Spencer, *A New, Authentic, and Complete History of England, from the First Settlement of Brutus in this Island, Upwards of A Thousand Years before the Time of Julius Caesar, to Year 1795* (London: A. Hogg, 1794), 30.

40. Ibid.

41. Henry Charles Coote, *The Romans of Britain* (London: Frederic Norgate, 1878), 159–70.

42. Ibid., 171.

43. Cornelius Tacitus, *The Agricola, and Germany of Tacitus* (London: MacMillan, 1868), 31, 55.

44. John Beddoe, *The Races of Britain: A Contribution to the Anthropology of Western Europe* (J. W. Anowsmith, 1885), 36.

45. Taylor, *A History of Germany from the Earliest Times to the Present Day* (New York: D. Appleton, 1894), 3.

46. C. Cornelius Tacitus, *A Treatise on the Situation, Manners, and Inhabitants, of Germany; and the Life of Agricola.* Translated into English by John Aikin. (Cambridge, Printed for W. Grant. Sold by J. Grant, Oxford; and T. & J. Allman, 1823), 115.

47. Caesar, 177.

48. Tacitus, ix.

49. Ibid.

50. Caesar, 218.

51. Tacitus's quote on Belgae, see Coote, 21–22.

52. Zimmermann, 20.

53. Ibid., 21.

54. Ibid., 170.

55. Tacitus, 55.

56. Wolfgang Menzel, *The History of Germany, from the Earliest Period to the Present Time* (London: Henry G. Bohn, 1852), 12.

57. J.G. Edgar, *Danes, Saxons, and Normans; or, Stories of Our Ancestors* (London: S. O. Beeton, 1863), 16–17.

58. J. J. A. Worsaae, *An Account of the Danes and Norwegians in England, Scotland, and Ireland* (London: Murray, 1852), 6–13.

59. Alice Morse Earle, *Customs and Fashions in Old New England* (New York: Charles Scribner's Sons, 1894), 28.

60. Benjamin Peirce, *A History of Harvard University: From Its Foundation in the Year 1636, to the Period of the American Revolution* (Cambridge: Brown, Shaltuck, and Company, 1833), 1.

61. Ibid., 3.

62. See Walter Moore, *Boston (Lincolnshire) and Its Surroundings: With an Account of the Pilgrim Fathers of New England* (London: Homeland Association, 1908), 33–34.

63. See Frederick Calvin Norton, "Biographies of the Governors of Connecticut," *The Connecticut Magazine, vol. 7*, 1901, 65.

64. Joseph Hopkins Twichell, *John Winthrop, First Governor of the Massachusetts Colony* (New York: Dodd, Mead, 1891), 14.

65. Ibid., 40.

66. G. Dyers, *History of the University and Colleges of Cambridge: Including Notices of the Founders and Eminent Men, Vol. 2* (London: Longman, Hurst, Rees, Orme, and Brown, 1814), 59, 64.

67. Ibid., 64–65.

68. James Terry White, *The National Cyclopaedia of American Biography, Vol. VI* (New York: James T. White & Company, 1896), 497.

69. Dyers, 343, 346–48.

70. John William and Edward Conybeare, *A History of Cambridge* (London: Elliot Stock, 1877), 192–93.

71. See Dorchester Antiquarian and Historical Society, 14–15.

72. Moore, 1908, 36.

73. Jacob Bailey Moore, *Lives of the Governors of New Plymouth and Massachusetts* (New York: Gates & Stedman, 1848), 336.

74. William Douglass, *A Summary, Historical and Political of the First Planting, Progressive Improvements, and Present State of the British Settlements in North America* (Boston, New England: R. Baldwin, 1755), 429.

75. George Fairbanks Partridge, *History of the Town of Bellingham, Massachusetts* (Bellingham by the town,1919), 1–3. In regard to his legal contributions, Partridge says that "he was repeatedly placed on a committee to draw up a code of fundamental laws based on the Bible, but the task was always put off because the magistrates avoided it in order not to transgress their charter; a no natural growth of the common law was safer to them," (3). He also posited that "he had a large share in the law making for the colony than any other man, unless Winthrop."

76. Norton, 66.

77. See "British Archaeological Association for Richard Saltonstall," *Journal of the British Archaeological Association 4* (1898): 23.

78. See *Calendar of State Papers* III–12.

79. Brooks, 43, 49.

Chapter 4

1. See *Calendar of State Papers,* xiii, xxii. This document says that "New England and Virginia are the parents of the Northern states of America."

2. See *The Public Records of the Colony of Connecticut [1636–1776]* (Hartford: Brown & Parsons, 1850), iii. Hammond J. Trumbull, the editor of the *Connecticut Public Records,* writes that "Governor Winthrop appointed noble personages and men of quality, interested in the said river, the commissioners named were Roger Williams, William Pincheon, John Steele, William Swaine, William Westwood, and Andrew Ward."

3. *The Public Statute Laws of the State of Connecticut. Book I* (Published by Authority of the General Court. (Hartford: Printed by Hudson and Goodwin, 1808.)

4. Joshua Wyman Wellman, *Descendants of Thomas Wellman of Lynn, Massachusetts* (Boston: Arthur Holbrook Wellman, 1918), 60.

5. Alonzo Lewis, *The History of Lynn, Including Nahant* (Boston: Samuel N. Dickson, 1844), 112.

6. Ibid.

7. Benjamin F. Thompson, *History of Long Island; Containing Account of the Discovery and Settlement* (New York: E. French, 1839), 438.

8. Epher Whitaker, *History of Southold, L.I. Its First Century* (Southold: Printed for the author, 1881), 27.

9. Ibid., 31.

10. Ibid., 32–33.

11. George Rogers Howell, *The Early History of Southampton, L.I.* (New York: J. N. Hollock, 1866), 9.

12. Settlers from Cambridge were dissatisfied due to the political climate of the time. Accordingly, they felt that the inhabitants of Boston were favored in tax rates. In their view, inhabitants of Cambridge paid more taxes than their brethren in Massachusetts. These complaints have been recorded by New England historians. There is reason to believe that their departure to Connecticut was due to these complaints.

13. John Winthrop, Winthrop's Journal "History of New England," 1630-1649, vol.1 (New York: Charles Scribner's Sons, 1908).

14. Convers Francis, *An Historical Sketch of Watertown, in Massachusetts, from the first settlement of the town to the close of Its Second Century* (Cambridge: EW.Metcalf and Company, 1830).

15. Dorchester Antiquarian and Historical Society, 63-64.

16. John Winthrop, Winthrop's Journal "History of New England," 1630–1649, Vol. 1 (New York: Charles Scribner's Sons, 1908), 74. The inhabitants of Watertown were ordered to pay eight pounds of the sixty pounds required for the fortification of Newtown. After the refusal of the inhabitants of Watertown to fulfill this order, a warrant was sent to them by the governor and the assistants at Boston. The pastor and elders of Watertown were also involved in this case. At the time when Massachusetts Bay officials convened in a meeting to resolve the issue, the pastor and elder of Watertown were present.

17. Ibid., 124.

18. Ibid., 108.

19. Ibid., 128.

20. Ibid., 132. Governor Winthrop listed the following reasons for their removal: the fruitfulness and commodiousness of Connecticut, and the danger of having it possessed by others, Dutch or English. In addition to listing these few reasons, Winthrop indicated his fear for the removal of the inhabitants of Newton to Connecticut. He lamented that the inhabitants of Newton and those of other towns were one body, and they were all determined to work for the welfare of the Commonwealth.

21. Ibid., 133.

22. William Bradford, *History of Plymouth Plantation* (Boston: Little, Brown, 1856), 338.

23. Ibid., 339. See the letter of Jonathan Brewster of July 6, 1635, to Governor William Bradford regarding the arrival of Bay men to Connecticut.

24. See Dorchester Antiquarian and Historical Society, 90.

25. Ibid., 35.

26. Ibid., 92.

27. Ibid., 101.

28. Winthrop, 165.

29. Ibid., 231.

30. See Walter Allen, "New Haven," *New England Magazine*, Vol. 20, 1899, 481.

31. Roger Williams was settled in Massachusetts when he immigrated to the colony. According to Salem local historians, he resided in that city for a time before being banished by the officials of the Massachusetts Bay Colony. In Salem, he was an assistant pastor. However, his opinions were perceived as dangerous to the authorities and the magistrates. Like Williams, Samuel Gorton faced the same fate. Gorton, a preacher from London, had different religious views, which offended the Massachusetts Bay Colony's Puritans.

32. Oliver Payson Fuller, *The History of Warwick, Rhode Island, From Its Settlement in 1642 to the Present Time* (Providence: Angell, Burlingame & Company, Printers), 1875, 8.

33. Edgar Mayhew Bacon, *Narragansett Bay: Its History and Romantic Associations and Picturesque Setting* (New York: G. P. Putnam's Sons), 1904, 33.

34. Isaac William Stuart, *Hartford in the Olden Time: Its First Thirty Years* (Hartford: F. A. Brown), 1853, 10.

35. Frederic Calvin Norton, "Biographies of the Governors of Connecticut," *Connecticut Magazine*, Vol.7, 1901, 59.

Chapter 5

1. Stuart, 233. Stuart praised the efforts of Rev. Roger Ludlow in codifying the Code of 1650 for the colony of Connecticut.

2. See *Records of the Company of the Massachusetts Bay in New England, Vol. 1* (Cambridge: Bolles and Houghton), 1850, lxix.

3. The Massachusetts Bay Company ordered Samuel Skelton and Francis Bright to form a government in Salem consisting of thirteen persons. In the same order, they were permitted to included old planters in that government. It is prudent to stipulate that members of this government were also lawmakers.

4. See the Company's Second General Letter on Instructions to Endecott and His Council of May 28, 1629, written in London. *Records of the Company of the Massachusetts Bay in New England, From 1628 to 1641. As Contained in the First Volume of the Archives of the Commonwealth of the Massachusetts* (Cambridge: Bolles and Houghton), 1850, 96.

5. See Thomas Williams Bicknell, *The History of the State of Rhode Island and Providence Plantations, Vol. 2* [New York]: American Historical Society, 1920, 432. Bicknell says that in 1640, the towns united in a well-ordered union styled a "Democracie." He went on to note that a governor, a deputy governor, four assistants, a secretary, a treasurer, and constables were elected to govern this first republic of the world, "a popular government."

6. See *Records of the Colony of Rhode Island and Providence Plantations, in New England: 1636–1663*. Vol.1 (Providence: A.C. Greene and Brothers, state printers), 1856, 52.

7. Bicknell, 431–32.

8. See *Records of the Colony of Rhode Island and Providence Plantations*, 52.

9. Ibid., 63. *Records of Providence* reveals that "elders were chosen to the

place of Eldership. They were to assist the judge in the execution of justice and judgement in regulating and ordering of all offences and offenders."

10. See *Records of the Colony of Rhode Island and Providence Plantations*, 63.

11. Ibid., 64.

12. Ibid., 87.

13. See *Records of the Colony of Rhode Island and Providence Plantations*, 14. On August 10, 1636, Roger Williams and his associates met together and formed a government for the welfare of the plantation. In a similar manner, Williams, with the rest of his associates, made an order that declared that no man should be molested for his conscience. This law is ample evidence that Roger Williams and his associates had legislative power.

14. George Washington Greene, *A Short History of Rhode Island* (Providence: J.A. & R.A. Reid), 1877, 18.

15. Bicknell, 432.

16. See *The Public Statute Laws of Connecticut, Vol. 1* (Hartford: Hudson and Goodwin), 1808, iv.

17. See *Laws and Acts of Her Majesties Colony of Rhode Island, and Providence Plantations made from the First Settlement in 1636 to 1705* (Providence, Rhode Island: Sidney S. Rider and Burnett Rider), 1896, vi.

18. Winthrop, 151.

19. Emory Washburn, *Sketches of the Judicial History of Massachusetts from 1630 to the Revolution in 1775* (Boston: Charles C. Little and James Brown), 1840, 22.

20. See Body of Liberties in *The Harvard Classics, Vol. 43*. P.F. (Collier & Son, 1910), 79.

21. See John F. Cronin, *Records of the Court of Assistants of the Colony of the Massachusetts Bay, 1630–1692, Vol. 1* (Boston: Published by the County of Suffolk, 1901), iv. According to *Records of the Court of Assistants*, during the early years of the Massachusetts Bay Colony, the powers and duties of the governor and the assistants sitting as a Court of Assistant for the trial of causes, civil and criminal, were not distinguished from the powers and duty of the same magistrates acting in the executive and legislative capacities under the charter.

22. Ibid.

23. See *Records of the Court of Assistants of the Colony of Massachusetts Bay 1630–1692, Vol. 2* (Boston: Published by the County of Suffolk), 1914.

24. Thomas Hutchinson, *The History of Massachusetts* (Salem: Thomas C. Cushing, 1795), 30.

25. Ibid.

26. Ibid.

27. See *The Public Records of the Colony of Connecticut [1636–1776]*, 21–25.

28. William R. Staples, *The Proceedings of the First General Assembly of "The Incorporation of Providence Plantations," and the Code of Laws Adopted by that Assembly, in 1647. With Notes Historical and Explanatory* (Providence: Charles Burnett, Jr.), 1847, x.

29. Ibid., ix.

30. Tacitus, 34–37.

31. Menzel, 7, 16, 35.

32. M. Guizot and Andrew K. Scoble, *History of the Origin of Representative Government in Europe* (London: Henry G. Bohn, 1861), 46.

33. Ibid., 47.

34. See Tacitus and James Kendrick, *Germany, and Agricola of Tacitus. The Oxford Translation Revised with Notes. With A Brief Introduction by James Kendrick* (New York: Translation Publishing Company, Inc., 1922), 16.

35. George William Spencer, *A New, Authentic, and Complete History of England, from the First Settlement of Brutus in this Island, Upwards of a Thousand Years before the Time of Julius Caesar to the Year, 1795* (London, Alexander Hogg, 1794), 30. Spencer writes that "the chief of the Germans was subject to the regulations of the states."

36. See the Company's Second General Letter on Instructions to Endecott and His Council, 96.

37. Ibid.

38. Hutchinson, 30.

39. Ibid., 36.

40. See *The Charters and General Laws of the Colony and Province of Massachusetts Bay* (Boston: T.E. Wait and Co., 1814), 97.

41. Ibid.

42. Joseph Willard, *Address to the Members of the Bar of Worcester County, Massachusetts, October 2, 1829* (Lancaster: Carter, Andrews, and Company, 1830), 15.

43. William Waller Hening, *The Statutes at Large: Being A Collection of All the Laws of Virginia, from the First Session of Legislative, in the Year 1619, Vol. 1* (New York: R.W. & G. Bartow, 1823), 112.

44. *The Charters and General Laws of the Colony and Province of the Massachusetts Bay*, 88.

45. *The Charter and General Laws of the Colony and Province of Massachusetts Bay*, 89.

46. See *The Public Records of the Colony of Connecticut [1636–1776]*, 22–24.

47. Hutchinson, 39.

48. Willard, 15.

49. See *Records of the Colony of Rhode Island and Providence Plantations*, iii.

50. Jeremy Belknap, *The History of New Hampshire* (Dover.: S. C. Stevens and Ela & Wadleigh, 1831), 453. The General Laws and Liberties of the Province of New Hampshire were enacted under the administration of President John Cutt.

51. See *Records of the Courts of Assistants of the Colony of the Massachusetts Bay, 1630–1692* (Boston: Court of Assistants, 1904), vii.

52. William Henry Whitmore, *A Bibliographical Sketch of the Laws of the Massachusetts Colony from 1630 to 1686: in which are Included the Body of Liberties of 1641, and the Records of the Court of Assistants, 1641–1644, Arranged to Accompany the Reprint of the Laws of 1660 and of 1672* (Boston: Rockwell and Churchill, 1890), 15.

53. See *Records of the Governor and Company of Massachusetts Bay in Massachusetts, Vol. III* (Boston: William White: Printer to the Commonwealth, 1854), 74.

54. See *Records of Governor and Company of the Massachusetts Bay in New England: M.2. 1661–1674, Vol. 4* (Boston: William White: Printer to the Commonwealth, 1854), 219. People assigned to the framing a blasphemy law were Mr. Nowell, Captain Atherton, Captain Thomas Clark, Captain Eleazer Lusher, and Mr. Edward Jackson, along with some reverend elders.

55. See *The Public Statute Laws of the State of Connecticut, Vol. 1* (Hartford: Hudson and Goodwin, 1808), iv.

56. Ibid., viii

57. Ibid.

58. Menzel, 16, 163.

59. William H. Whitmore, *The Colonial Laws of Massachusetts. Reprinted from the Edition of 1660, with the Supplements to 1672. Containing Also the Body of Liberties of 1641* (Boston: Rockwell & Churchill, 1889), 16.

60. George Blaxland, *Code Legum Anglicanarum: Or A Digest of Principles of English Law: Arranged in the Order of the Code of Napoleon* (London: Henry Butterwooth, 1839), 11.

61. Ibid.

62. Spencer, 34.

63. Blaxland, 11.

64. Spencer, 40.

65. Winthrop, 151. Winthrop writes that "the deputies having conceived great danger to our state, in regard that our magistrates, for want of positive laws, in many cases, might proceed according to their discretions, it was agreed that some men should be appointed to frame a body grounds laws, in

resemblance to a Magna Carta, which, being allowed by some of the ministers, and the general court, should be received for fundamental laws."

66. Whitmore, xvi.

67. Dwight Loomis, *The Judicial and Civil History of Connecticut* (Boston: The Boston Calhoun Historical Company, 1895).

68. *Law and Acts of Her Majesties Colony of Rhode Island*, vi.

69. *Laws and Acts of Her Majesties Colony of Rhode Island*, v.

70. For *the codification of New Hampshire laws, see New Hampshire. Supreme Court, The New Hampshire Reports, vol.3.* Capital Offset Company, 1874, 108-109.

71. See *Laws of New Hampshire: Province Period, 1679–1702* (Manchester: John B. Clarke Company, 1904), xlvii.

72. Ibid.

73. Edward Cooke, *The Second Part of the Institutes of the Laws of England* (London, Printed for E. and R. Brooke, 1797), 569.

74. Ibid.

75. T. Cunningham, *The Practice of a Justice of Peace: Containing the Status which gives Jurisdiction to the Magistrate* (London: Printed by E. Richard and C. Lintot, 1757), 326.

76. See *Records of the Governor and Company of the Massachusetts Bay in New England: Part 2, 1661–1674, Vol. 4* (Boston: W. White, 1854), 22–23.

77. See *Public Statutes Laws of Connecticut, Vol. 1* (Hartford: Printed by Hudson and Goodwin, 1808), vi.

78. Elizabeth Hibbell Schenck, *The History of Fairfield, Fairfield County, Connecticut: From the Settlement of the Town in 1639 to 1818* (New York: Published by the author, 1889), 15.

79. Weeden, 79–80.

80. Ibid.

81. See Moore, 36. Richard Bellingham was record keeper of the town of Boston from 1625 to 1633.

82. See "Act for Keeping Records of Judgements and Evidence of 1632," in *The Charters and General Laws of the Colony and Province of Massachusetts Bay* (Boston: T. E. Wait and Co., 1814), 43.

83. J. Luther Ringwalt, *American Encylopaedia of Printing* (Philadelphia: Menamin & Ringwalt, 1871), 132.

84. J. Bosworth, *The Elements of Anglo-Saxon Grammar, with Copious Notes* (London: Printed for Harding Mavor, and Lepard, 1823), 16–21.

85. Ibid.

86. Ibid.

87. See *Library of Universal Knowledge. A Report of the Last (1880) Edinburgh and London Edition of Chambers's Encyclopaedia, Vol. 2* (New York: American Book Exchange, 1880), 186.

88. Ibid.

89. Ibid.

90. See *Records of the Governor and Company of the Massachusetts Bay in New England, Vol. 2 1642–1649* (Boston: William White Press, 1853), 22.

91. Ibid., 28.

92. Ibid., 212.

93. Ibid., 262.

94. Ibid., 286.

95. Ibid., 35.

96. Isaiah Thomas, *The History of Printing in America, Vol. 2* (New York: Burt Franklin, 1874), 318.

Chapter 6

1. Charles Brooks, *History of the Town of Medford, Middlesex County, Massachusetts: From Its First Settlement in 1630 to 1855* (Boston: Rand, Avery), 35, 46, 103, 377.

2. *Records of the Colony and Plantation of New Haven, from 1638 to 1649* (Hartford: Case, Tiffany and Company, 1857), 44. In 1640, in New Haven, it was ordered that workmen shall not work above four months in winter. They had to work eight hours diligently each day to be paid for a full day's work.

3. *The Compact with the Charter and Laws of the Colony of New Plymouth, New Plymouth Colony* (Boston: Dutton and Wentworth, Printers to the States, 1836), 28.

4. See "Full Text: Donald Trump 2016 RNC Draft Speech Transcript," Politico, July 21, 2016, https://www.politico.com/story/2016/07/full-transcript-donald-trump-nomination-acceptance-speech-at-rnc-225974.

5. Alfred Henry Ruegg, *The Laws Regulating the Relation of Employer and Workman in England* (London: William Clowes and Son, 1905), 12-14.

6. See Thomas Ruggles, *The History of Poor: Their Rights, Duties, and Laws Respecting Them. In a Series of Letters* (London: W. Richardson, 1797), 20. Ruggles writes that "according to the statutes, a bailiff was allowed 13 s. 4. a year; a master-hind, 10 s.; a carter, 10 s.; shepherd, 10 s.; oxherd, 6 s. 8.; a plough-driver, 7s."

7. Ibid., 21.

8. Ruegg, 13-14.

9. George Roberts, *The Social History of the People of the Southern Counties of England in Past Centuries* (London: Longman, Brown, Green, Longmans & Robert, 1856), 205.

10. John Reeves, *History of the English Law, From the Time of the Saxons, to the End of the Reign of Elizabeth, Vol. 5* (London: Printed by A. Strahans, 1829), 6.

11. Ibid.

12. Ibid., 11.

13. Ibid. Reeves notes that "carters, ploughmen, and other servants were to serve by the whole year, or by other usual terms, and not by the day, c.1."

14. Roberts, 194.

15. Trail, 550.

16. Michael Oppenheim, *Naval Accounts and Inventories of the Reign of Henry VII: 1485–8 and Navy Records Society* (London: Navy Records Society, 1896), liv.

17. See *Records of the Company of the Massachusetts Bay in New England, From 1628 to 1641, Vol.1* (Cambridge: Bolles and Houghton, 1850), 100.

18. Ibid.

19. Lewis, 72.

20. Ibid.,

21. See *Records of the Court of Assistants of the Colony of Massachusetts Bay 1630–1692, Vol. 2*, 12.

22. Ibid. Carpenters, joiners, and other artificers, including workmen were freely allowed to negotiate their wages at reasonable price.

23. See *Records of the Courts of Assistants of the Colony of Massachusetts Bay 1630–1692, Vol. 2*, 12. The Court ordered that the wages of carpenters, joiners, and other artificers, and workmen were now to be left free at liberty as men shall reasonably agree.

24. William B. Weeden, *Economic and Social History of New England, 1620–1789* (Houghton, Mifflin and Company, 1890), 83.

25. Ibid.

26. Winthrop, 112.

27. Ibid.

28. Ibid.

29. See *The Public Records of the Colony of Connecticut [1636–1776]*, 65.

30. *Records of the Colony of Rhode Island and Providence Plantations, in New England: 1636–1663*, 307.

31. See *The Charters and General Laws of the Colony and Province of Massachusetts Bay*, 57.

32. See *Records of the Court of Assistants of the Colony of the Massachusetts Bay 1630–1692*, 37.

33. Stuart, 111.

34. Winthrop, 102.

35. Ibid.

36. Charles M. Endecott, *Memoir of John Endecott, First Governor of the Colony of Massachusetts Bay* (Salem: Printed at the Observed Office, 1847), 77.

37. Loomis, 113.

38. Ibid., 113–114.

39. Edward Rodolphus Lambert, *History of the Colony of New Haven* (New Haven: Hitchcock & Stafford, 1838), 32.

40. Loomis, 120.

41. *A Report of the Commissioners Containing Charlestown Land. Records, 1638–1802*, second edition (Boston: Rockwell and Churchill, City Printers, 1883), 13.

42. Richard Frothingham, *The History of Charlestown, Massachusetts* (Boston: C. Little and James Brown, 1845), 135.

43. *The Public Records of the Colony of Connecticut [1636–1776]*, 11.

44. See *The Oppression of Wages, Third Annual Report of the Bureau of Labor Statistics, of the State of Connecticut, for the Year Ending November 30, 1887* (Hartford: Press of the Case, Lockwood of Co., 1877), 131.

45. Weeden, 83.

46. Ibid.

47. *Records of the Court of Assistants of the Colony of the Massachusetts Bay 1630–1692, Vol. 2*, 131.

48. Ibid., 131.

49. Ibid., 255.

50. Edward H. Savage, *A Chronological History of the Boston Watch and Police, from 1631 to 1865: Together with the Collections of a Boston Police Officer or Boston by Daylight and Gaslight, from the Diary of an Officer Fifteen Years in the Service* (Boston: Published and Sold by the Author, 1865).

51. *The Public Records of the Colony of Connecticut [1636–1776]*, 81.

52. *The Charters and General Laws of the Colony and Province of the Massachusetts Bay*, 101.

53. Ibid., 101–3.

54. See *Records of the Court of Assistants of the Colony of the Massachusetts Bay 1630–1692, Vol. 2*, 9.

55. Ibid., 13.

Chapter 7

1. See *Records of the Colony of New Plymouth, in New England: Laws, 1623–1682* (Boston: Press of W. White, 1861), 4.

2. Ibid.

3. See *The Compact with the Charter and Laws of the Colony of New Plymouth*, 35.

4. Weeden, 40.

5. Brooks, 46.

6. Weeden, 40.

7. Ibid.

8. Winthrop, 20.

9. Morse Earle, 194.

10. Samuel Adams Drake, *Old Landmarks and Historic Personages of Boston* (Boston: James R. Osgood and Company, 1873), 14.

11. For the regulation regarding oppression of wages, see the *Third Annual Report of the Bureau of Labor Statistics, of the State of Connecticut, for the year Ending November 30, 1887*, 135.

12. Ibid., 74.

13. Winthrop, 315.

14. Ibid.

15. See *Records of Massachusetts, Vol. IV. Part I 1650–1660* (Boston: William White, 1854), 302.

16. *Records of the Court of Assistants of the Colony of Massachusetts Bay 1630–1692, Vol. 2*, 131.

17. See *The Charters and General Laws of the Colony and Province of Massachusetts Bay*, 109, 110. In Salem, two fairs were held every year on the last fourth day of the third month and the last fourth day of the seventh month. In Watertown, two fairs were held each year on the sixth day of the fourth month and the first day of the seventh month. In Dorchester, two fairs were open a year, on the fourth third day of the first month and the last fourth day of the eighth month.

18. *The Compact with the Charter and Laws of the Colony of New Plymouth*, 63.

19. See *Records of the Colony and Plantation of New Haven, from 1638 to 1649*, 130.

20. *The Public Records of the Colony of Connecticut [1636–1776]*, 125.

21. See *The Compact with the Charter and Laws of the Colony of New Plymouth*, 61.

22. Felt, 97.

23. See *Records of the Governor and Company of Massachusetts Bay in New England: 1644–1651, Vol. 3* (Boston: W. White, 1854), 132.

24. See *Third Annual Report of the Bureau of Labor Statics, of the State of Connecticut, for the Year Ending November 30, 1887*, 129–30.

25. *Records of the Court of Assistants of the Colony of Massachusetts Bay 1630–1692, Vol.2*, 85.

26. Ibid., 84.

27. *The Compact, Charter and Laws of the Colony of New Plymouth*, 73.

28. Weeden, 102.

29. *The Compact, Charter and Laws of the Colony of New Plymouth*, 80.

30. See *Records of the Court of Assistants of the Colony of Massachusetts Bay, 1630–1692*, 8.

31. M. Hartwell, Edward W. McGlenen, and Edward O. Skelton, *Boston and Its Story 1630-1915* (Boston: City of Boston Printing Department, 1916), 51.

32. See *The Compact, Charter and Laws of the Colony of New Plymouth*, 62.

33. Ibid., 59.

34. *The Public Records of the Colony of Connecticut [1636–1776]*, 71.

35. See *Records of the Governor and Company of Massachusetts Bay in New England, Vol. 2*, 170.

36. See *The Charters and General Laws of the Colony and Province of Massachusetts Bay*, 111.

37. See *Calendar of State Papers, Colonial Series, America and West Indies, 1681–1695* (London: Printed for Her Majesty's Stationary Office, 1898), 44.

38. See *The Charters and General Laws of the Colony and Province of Massachusetts Bay*, 111.

39. See "Post Office," in *Collections of the Massachusetts Historical Society, Vol. 7 of the Third Series* (Boston: Charles C. Little and James Brown, 1838), 48–50.

40. Ibid.

41. Ibid.

Chapter 8

1. See Arthur C. Boyden, "Development of Education in Massachusetts," *The Commonwealth of Massachusetts Bulletin of the Department of Education* [Volume], no. 5 (1930).

2. Martin Bladen, trans., *Caius Ivlius Caesar's Commentaries of His Wars in Gaul, and Civil War with Pompey* (London: Arlus Hiritius, or Oppius, &c., 1737), 114–15.

3. Nicholas Carlisle, *Concise Description of the Endowed Grammar Schools in England and Wales; Ornamented with Engravings, Vol. 1* (London: W. Bulmer and Co., 1818), ix.

4. Ibid., xii.

5. Arthur Francis Leach, *The Schools of Medieval England* (New York: The MacMillan Company, 1915), vii.

6. Thomas Wright, *Anglo-Saxon Period* (London: J.W. Parker, 1842), 64.

7. Bede and J. A. Giles, *The Ecclesiastical History of the English Nation. Translated from the Latin of Venerable Bede. To Which is Prefixed a Life of the Author* (London: H. G. Bohn, 1849).

8. A.D. Bayne, *Royal Illustrated History of Eastern England; Civil, Military, Political, and Ecclesiastical* (Great Yarmouth : James Macdonald & Co., 1873), 316.

9. Ibid., 296.

10. Ibid., 80.

11. Leach, 113.

12. Ibid., 114.

13. Carlisle, 101.

14. Ibid., 191.

15. Ibid., 322.

16. Roger Ascham, *The Scholemaster* (London: Higginbotham and Co., 1877), 1–7. Ascham has been credited with being the pioneer and architect of the teaching of his native literature. He attended Cambridge University and was a teacher to Queen Elizabeth. He taught the queen how to read and write Latin and Greek.

17. Josiah Quincy, *The History of Harvard University, Vol. 1* (Cambridge: John Owen, 1840), 9.

18. See *History of the Hopkins Funds, Grammar School and Academy, in Hadley, Massachusetts* (Amherst: Amherst Record Press, 1890), 38.

19. Carlisle, 379. Carlisle notes that "by the original charter, twenty of the principal inhabitants of the town of Sherborne were appointed Governors, constituted a Body Corporate, and empowered to elect new governors as often as vacancies should happen."

20. See *The Company's First General Letter of Instructions to Endecott and His Council written in Gravesend, the 17th of April in 1629. Records of the Company of the Massachusetts Bay in New England: From 1628 to 1641. As Contained in the First Volume of the Archives of the Commonwealth of Massachusetts, Vol. 1* (Cambridge: Bolles and Houghton, 1850), 93.

21. Ibid.

22. Ibid.

23. Ibid., 99.

24. *The Charters and General Laws of the Colony and Province of Massachusetts Bay*, 73.

25. James Otis, *Ruth of Boston. A Story of the Massachusetts Bay Colony* (New York: American Book Company, 1910), 126.

26. Ibid.

27. Tacitus, *The Works of Tacitus, The Oxford Translation; Revised with Notes, Vol. 2, The History, Germany, Agricola and Dialogue on Orators* (London: George Bell & Sons, 1889), 412.

28. A. E. Lawson Lowe, *Historical Record of the Royal Forester; Or Nottinghamshire Regiment of Militia* (London: W. Mitchell & Co., Military Publishers, 1872), 3.

29. Ibid.

30. Ibid.

31. Charles Brooks, *History of the Town of Medford, Middlesex County, Massachusetts: From Its Settlement in 1630 to 1855* (Boston: Rand, Every, 1886), 173.

32. Ibid., 173–74.

33. Ibid.

34. Ibid., 175.

35. Ibid.

36. *The Public Records of the Colony of Connecticut [1636–1776]*, 4.

37. Ibid.

38. Ibid.

39. Isaac W. Stuart, *Hartford in the Olden Time: Its First Thirty Years.* (Hartford: F.A. Brown), 65.

40. Jacob Abbott, *Richard II* (New York and London: Harper & Brothers Publishers, 1900), 296.

41. John Strype, *The Life of the Learned Sir John Cheke. First Instructor, Afterwards Secretary of State to King Edward VI* (Oxford: Clarendon Press, 1821), 1.

42. Ibid., 5.

43. Charles John Smith, *Autographs of Royal, Noble, Learned and Remarkable Conspicuous in English History* (London: J. B. Nichols and Son, 1829), vi.

44. See *The Mirror of Literature, Amusement, and Instruction: New Series, Vol. 3* (London: Cunningham and Mortimer, 1843), 153.

45. Brooks, 278.

46. Thomas B. Stockwell, *A History of Public Education in Rhode Island from 1636 to 1876* (Providence: Providence Press Company, Printers to the City and State, 1876), 1.

47. Morse Earle, 31.

48. Brooks, 278.

49. Ibid., 281.

50. Otis, 119.

51. Ibid.

52. Ibid.

53. Charles H. Walcott, *Concord in the Colonial Period. Being a History of the Town of Concord, Massachusetts, 1635–1689* (Boston: Estes and Lauriat, 1884), 129.

54. See Boyden, 4.

55. Harlan Updegraff, *The Origin of the Moving School in Massachusetts* (New York: Columbia University Press, 1907), 137.

56. Ibid.

57. See *Records of the Governor and Company of the Massachusetts Bay in New England, Vol. 2,* 8.

58. Henry Suzzallo, *The Rise of Local School Supervision in Massachusetts (The School Committee, 1635–1827)* (New York: Teachers College, Columbia University, 1906), 6.

59. Boyden, 4.

60. See Otis, 113.

61. Ibid.

62. Ibid.

63. Ibid.

64. Caleb Hopkins Snow, *A History of Boston: The Metropolis of Massachusetts, from Its Origin to the Present Period; with some Account of the Environs* (Boston: Abel Bowen, 1828), 348.

65. Otis, 114.

66. Ibid.

67. Ibid.

68. Felt, 523.

69. C. K. Dillaway, *History of the Grammar School, or the Free School in Roxburie* (Roxbury: John Backap, 1860), 175.

70. Snow, 348.

71. Oliver Ayer Robert, *History of the Military Company of the Massachusetts, Now Called the Ancient and Honorable Artillery* (Boston: Alfred Mudge & Son, Printers, 1895), 149.

72. Francis S. Drake, *The Town of Roxbury: Its Memorable Persons and Places. Its History and Antiquities with Numerous Illustrations of Its Old Landmarks and Noted Personages* (Roxbury: Published by the author, 1878), 160.

73. Ibid., 161.

74. See *Publication of the Colonial Society of Massachusetts, Transactions Colonial Society of Massachusetts* (Boston: Published by the Society, 1805), 117–18.

75. Ibid.

76. Ibid.

77. Drake, 194.

78. Ibid., 169, 187.

79. See General Joshua L. Chamberlain, *Universities and Their Sons. History, Influence, and Characteristics of American Universities with Biographical Sketches and Portraits of Alumni and Recipients of Honorary Degrees* (Boston: R. Herndon Company, 1900), 320.

80. Ibid., 172.

81. Ibid., 370.

82. See G. B. Emerson, "Education in Massachusetts," Report of the Commission of Education for the Year 1896–97, Vol. 2 (Washington: Government Printing Office, 1898), 1169.

83. Felt, 112.

84. Ibid., 127.

85. Ibid., 165.

86. Endecott, 77.

87. Felt, 241–43.

88. See Dorchester Antiquarian and Historical Society, 160.

89. Ibid., 141, 160, 208.

90. See Dorchester Antiquarian and Historical Society, 437.

91. Ibid., 165.

92. John J. Currier, *History of Newbury, Mass., 1635–1902* (Boston: Damrell & Upham, 1902), 395.

93. Ibid., 396–97.

94. Ibid.

95. Francis Jackson, *History of the Early Settlement of Newton, County of Middlesex, Massachusetts from 1639 to 1800* (Boston: Stacy and Richardson, 1854), 64.

96. See *The Charters and General Laws of the Colony and Province of Massachusetts Bay*, 186.

97. Ibid.

98. Ibid.

99. Ibid.

100. Ibid., 187.

101. Ibid.

102. Ibid.

103. Don Gleason Hill, *The Early Records of the Town of Dedham, Massachusetts 1636–1659 in Three Volumes* (Dedham, Mass.: Printed at Office of Dedham Transcript, 1892), 15.

104. Ibid., 16.

105. Suzzallo, 6.

106. Richard Frothingham Jr. *The History of Charlestown, Massachusetts* (Boston: Charles C. Little and Jones Brown, 1845), 177–84.

107. Samuel A. Bates, *The Early Schools of Braintree* (South Braintree: Frank A. Bates, 1899), 3.

108. Ibid., 5–6.

109. See *Weymouth Historical Society, Sketch of the Town of Weymouth, Massachusetts from 1622 to 1884* (Weymouth: Gilbert Nash, Published by the Town of Weymouth, under the Auspices of the Weymouth Historical Society, 1885), 125.

110. Ibid., 125–26.

111. Lucius R. Paige, *History of Cambridge, Massachusetts, 1630-1877* (Boston: H. O. Houghton Company, 1877), 365–66.

112. Jackson, 64.

113. Ibid.

114. Ibid., 64.

115. Samuel Hopkins Emery, *History of Taunton, Massachusetts from Its Settlement to the Present Time* (Syracuse, N.Y.: D. Mason & Co. Publisher, 1893), 276, 282, 283.

116. Ibid.

117. Solomon Lincoln Jr., *History of the Town of Hingham, Plymouth County, Massachusetts* (Hingham: Cobel Gill, Jr. and Farmer and Brown, 1827), 20.

118. Ibid.

119. Edward Elias Atwater, *History of the Colony of New Haven to Its Absorption into Connecticut* (New Haven: Printed for the Author, 1881), 263.

120. Ibid., 262.

121. Alfred Andrews, *Genealogical History of John and Mary Andrews, Who Settled in Farmington, Conn., 1640* (Chicago: Andrews & Co., 1872).

122. Hammond J. Trumbull, *The Memorial History of Hartford County, Connecticut 1633–1884 in 2 Vols.* (Boston: Edward L. Osgood Publisher, 1886), 640.

123. See *A Handbook of American Private Schools. An Annual Survey Fifth Edition* (Boston: Porter E. Sargent, 1919), 13.

124. Richard M. Bayles, *History of Newport County, Rhode Island: From the year 1638 to the Year 1887, Including the Settlement of Its Towns, and Their Subsequent Progress* (New York: Preston & Co., 1888), 58.

125. Bicknell, 653.

126. Ibid.

127. See Swansea, Massachusetts.

128. Stockwell, 9.

129. See *A Handbook of American Private Schools. An Annual Survey Fifth Edition*, 11.

130. Boyden, 4.

131. Sarah Loring Bailey, *Historical Sketches of Andover (Comprising the Present Towns of North Andover and Andover), Massachusetts* (Boston: Houghton, Mifflin, and Company, 1880), 517.

132. See Rollo La Verne Lyman, "English Grammar in American Schools before 1850. A Dissertation Submitted to the Faculty of the Graduate School of Arts and Literature in Candidacy for the Degree of Doctor of Philosophy Department," Reprinted from Department of the Interior, Bureau of Education, Bulletin, no.12 (1921, 1922).

133. Suzzallo, 1.

134. John J. Currier, *History of Newbury, Mass., 1635–1902* (Boston: Damerell & Upham, 1902), 395.

135. See Allen, 486.

136. See *Records of the Governor and Company of the Massachusetts Bay in New England*, 30.

137. Ibid.

138. See *Records of the Governor and Company of the Massachusetts Bay in New England: Pt. 2, Vol. 4. Part I. 1650–1660* (Boston: M. White, 1854), 12.

139. See *The Charters and General Laws of the Colony and Province of Massachusetts Bay*, 52.

140. *Records of the Colony and Plantation of New Haven, from 1638 to 1649*, 216.

141. *Records of the Governor and Company of the Massachusetts Bay, Vol. IV*, 101.

142. Walcott, 130.

143. Ibid., 128.

144. See *The Hampshire Book Being Specimens of the Literature of the Granite State* (Nashville: Charles T. Gill, 1844), 254.

145. See Records of the Governor and Company of the Massachusetts Bay in New England:pt.2. 1661-1674, Vol. IV. W. White. Printer to the Commonwealth, 1854, 315.

146. Ibid., 279.

Bibliography

Archival Materials for the Massachusetts Bay Colony

A Report of the Record Commissioners Containing Charlestown Land. Records, 1638–1802, Second Edition. Boston: Rockwell and Churchill, City Printers, 1883.

Massachusetts Archives Collection Records (1629–1686). Historical Sketch-Colonial Period (1629–1686). Boston, See the website of the Secretary of the Commonwealth of Massachusetts.

Records of the Court of Assistants of the Colony of the Massachusetts Bay, 1630–1692. County of Suffolk: John F. Cromin, County of Suffolk, 1901.

Records of the Governor and Company of the Massachusetts Bay in New England, Vol. 1. Boston: Bollis and Houghton, 1850.

Records of the Governor and Company of the Massachusetts Bay in New England, Vol. 4. Boston: William White, 1854.

Records of the Governor and Company of the Massachusetts Bay in New England, Vol. 2. Boston: William White, 1853.

Records of the Governor and Company of the Massachusetts Bay in New England, Vol. 3. Boston: William White, 1854.

Records of the Governor and Company of the Massachusetts Bay in New England, Vol. 4. Boston: William White, 1854.

Second Report of the Record Commissioners of the City of Boston: Containing the Boston Records, 1634–1660, And the Book of Possessions, Second Edition. Boston: Rockwell and Churchill, City Printers, 1881.

The Charters and General Laws of the Colony and Province of Massachusetts Bay. Boston: T. E. Wait and Co., 1814.

The Compact with the Charter & Laws of the Colony of New Plymouth. Dutton & Wentworth, 1836. Three vols. Dedham, Mass.: Don Gleason Hill, Dedham, Mass., 1892.

The Colonial Laws of Massachusetts: Reprinted from the Edition of 1660, with the Supplements to 1672: Containing Also, the Body of Liberties of 1641. Boston: Rockwell and Churchill, City Printers, 1889.

School Document No. 15-1901. Annual Report of the School Committee of the City of
Boston. Boston: Municipal Printing Office, 1901.

Archival Materials for the Connecticut Colony

The Public Records of the Colony of Connecticut [1636–1776]. Hartford: Press of
the Case, 1850.
The Public Records of Connecticut Prior to the Union with New Haven Colony,
May, 1665. Hartford: Brown & Parsons, 1850.
Records of the Colony and Plantation of New Haven, from 1638 to 1649. Transcribed
and edited in Accordance of the General Assembly of Connecticut. Hartford: by
Case, Tiffany and Company, 1857.
The Code of 1650, Being a Compilation of the Earliest Laws and Orders of the Gen-
eral Court of Connecticut; Also, The Constitution, or Civil Compact, Entered into
and Adopted by the Towns of Windsor, Hartford, and Wethersfield in 1638–9. To
Which is added some Extracts from the Laws and Judicial Proceeding of New
Haven Colony Commonly called Blue Laws. Hartford: Silas Andrus, 1825.

Archival Materials for the
Rhode Island and Providence Plantations

Records of the Colony of Rhode Island and Providence Plantation in New England:
1636–1663. [Providence: A.C. Greene and Brothers, State Printers, 1856.
Laws and Acts of Her Majesties Colony of Rhode Island and Providence Plantations
Made from the First Settlement in 1636 to 1705. With Historical Introduction
by Sidner S. Rider. Providence, Rhode Island: Sidney S. Rider and Burnett
Ridder, 1896.

Archival Materials for Great Britain

Calendaer of State Papers: 9–] America and West Indies, 1574. Great Britain: Public
Record Office, Longman, 1860. See Grant for Newfoundland, Letter from
the king to the Lords Lieutenant of Cornwall, Somerset, Devon, and to the
cities of Bristol and Exeter for support of the migration movement to New
England.
Calendaer of State Papers, Colonial Series . . . : Preserved in the Public Record Office. Great Britain: Public Record Office, 1860.

A. E. Lawson Lowe, A. E. *Historical Record of the Royal Sherwood Foresters; or Nottingham Regiment of Militia.* By Capt. London: W. Mitchell & Co., Military Publishers, 1872.

Selection of Reports and Papers of the House of Commons: Poor, [1], Vol. 39, 1836. See Edward III. on excessive wages.

London Society, Vol. 7, 1865. See discussion on Bristol Merchants and Cabotos.

The Journal of All the Parliaments during the Reign of Queen Elizabeth: Both of the House of Lords and House of Commons. London: Printed for John Storley, 1682.

See *Records of the Council for New England. Press of J. Wilson & Son. 1867. Here the discussion on the incorporation of this association is noted.*

Naval Accounts and Inventories of the Reign of Henry VII: 1485-8 and 1495-7. Navy Records Society. 1896.

Journal of the British Archaeological Association, Vol. 4. British Archaeological Association. 1898. See Sir Richard Saltonstall.

The Geographical Journal, Vol. 9, Royal Geographical Society, 1897. " Fourth Centenary of the Voyage of John Cabot, 1497."

Report & Transactions, Vol. 14. Devonshire Association for the Advancement of Science, Literature and Art, 1882. Discussion about the Plymouth Company in England.

Printed Books

Abbott, Jacob. *Richard II.* New York and London, Harper & Brothers Publishers, 1900.

Adolguphus, John. *The Political State of the British Empire; Containing A General View of the Domestic and Foreign Possessions of the Crown: The Laws, Commerce, Revenue.* In four volume, *Vol. 3.* London: Printed for T. Cadell and W. Daviers, 1818.

Adams, Charles F. *History of Braintree, Massachusetts (1639–1708).* Cambridge: Printed at the Riverside Press, 1891.

Adams, Nathaniel. *Annals of Portsmouth.* Portsmouth, N.H.: Published by the Author, 1825.

Aikin, Lucy. *Memoirs of the Court of King Charles the First, Vol. 1.* London: Longman, Rees, Orne, Brown, Green and Longman, vol. 1, 1833.

Ames, Josephhn. *Typographical Antiquities; or the History of Printing in England, Scotland and Ireland, Vol. 1.* London, Printed for William Miller, Albermarle Publisher, 1810.

Anderson, Joseph. *The Town and City of Waterbury, Connecticut, Vol. 1*. New Haven: Price and Lee Company, 1896.

Andrews, Alfred. *Genealogy History of John and Mary Andrews, who Settled in Farmington, Connecticut, 1640*. Chicago: Andrews & Co., 1872.

Arbuthnot, John. *Tables of Ancient Coins, Weights and Measure: Explained and Exemplified in Several Dissertations*. London: Printed for J. Tonson, 1727.

Ascham, Roger, and J. T. Margoschis. *The Scholemaster*. London: Higginbotham and Co., 1877.

Atwater, Edward E. *History of the Colony of New Haven to Its Absorption into Connecticut*. New Haven: Published by the Author, 1881.

Bacon, Edgar M. *Narragansett Bay: Its History and Romantic Association and Picturesque Setting*. New York: G. P. Putnam' Sons, 1904.

Bacon, Francis. *Bacon's History of the Reign of King Henry VII*. Cambridge: University Press, 1885.

Bancroft, George. *History of the United States of America, from the Discovery of the Continent [to 1789] Vol.1*. Boston: Little, 1876.

Bancroft, George. *History of the Colonization of the United States*. Boston: C.C. Little and J. Brown, 1839.

———. *History of the United States of America, from the Discovery of the Continent [to 1789] Vol. 1*. Boston: Little Brown and Co., 1876.

Bates, Samuel A. *The Early Schools of Braintree*. South Braintree: Frank A. Bates, 1899.

Bayles, Richard M. *History of Newport County, Rhode Island:. From the Year 1638 to the Year 1887, Including the Settlement of Its Towns, and their Subsequent Progress*. New York: Preston & Co., 1888.

Bailey, Sarah L. *Historical Sketches of Andover (Comprising the Present Towns of North Andover and Andover), Massachusetts*. Boston: Houghton, Mifflin, and Company, 1880.

Bayne, A. D. *Royal Illustrated History of Eastern England, Civil, Military, Political, and Ecclesiastical*. Great Yarmouth: James Macdonald & Co., 1873.

Baynes, Thomas S. *The Encyclopaedia Britannica: A Dictionary of Arts, Sciences, and General Literature, Vol. 12*. Philadelphia: M. Sommerville, 1891.

Bede, Saint (The Venerable). *The Ecclesiastical History of the English Nation*. London: T. Meigham, 1723.

Beddoe, John. *The Races of Britain: A Contribution to the Anthropology of Western Europe*. Bristol: J. W. Arrnowsmith, 1885.

Belknap, Jeremy. *The History of New Hampshire*. Boston: Bradford and Reed, 1812.

Bell, Charles H. *History of the Town of Exeter, New Hampshire*. Exeter: The Quarter-Millennial Year, 1888.

Bicknell, Thomas W. *The History of the State of Rhode Island and Providence Plantations, Vol. 2*. New York: The American Historical Society, 1920.

Biddle, Richard. *A Memior of Sebastian Cabot: With a Review of the History of Maritime Discovery. Illustrated by Document from the Rolls, Now First Published*. London: Hurst, Chance, and Company, 1831.

Birch, Thomas. *Memoirs of the Reign of Queen Elizabeth, from the Year 1581 Till her Death*. London: Printed for A. Miller, 1754.

Blaxland, George. *Code Legun Anglicanarum, Or A Digest of Principles of English Law; Arranged in the Order of the Code Napoleon*. London: Henry Butterworth, 1839.

Blomefield, Francis. *Collectanea Cantabrigiensia, Or Collections Relating to Cambridge, University, Town, and County, Containing*. Norwich: Printed for the Author, 1751.

Bourne Henry, R. F. *English Merchants: Memoirs in Illustration of the Progress of British Commerce, Vol. 1*. London: R. Bentley, 1866.

Bosworth, J. *The Elements of Anglo-Saxon Grammar, with Copious Notes*. London: Printed for Harding, Mavor, and Lepard, 1823.

Bradford, William. *History of Plymouth Plantation*. Boston: Little, Brown, 1856.

Brooks, Charles. *History of the Town of Medford, Middlesex County, Massachusetts from Its First Settlement in 1630 to 1855*. Boston: Rand, Avery, 1886.

Brown, Alexander. *The First Republic in America*. Boston and New York: Houghton, Mifflin and Company, 1898.

Brown, John. *The Pilgrim Fathers of New England and their Puritan Successors*. New York: Fleming H. Revell Company, 1895.

Bush, George G. *History of Education in New Hampshire*. Washington: Government Printing Office, 1898.

Bush, George G. *Harvard the First American University*. Boston: Upham and Company, 1866.

Busch, Wilhelm. *England under the Tudors: King Henry VII, 1484–1509*. New York: B. Franklin, 1895. Translated from Germany by Alice M. Todd

Byington, Ezra H. *The Puritan in England and New England*. Boston: Roberts Brothers, 1897.

Caesar, Julius. *Julius Caesar's Commentaries on the Gaul War/with a dictionary and notes by E.A. Andrews*. Boston: Crockerker and Brewster, 1864.

Camden, William. *Annals, or, the Historie of the Most Renowned and Victorious Princess Elizabeth, Late Queen of England.* Translated into English by R.N. Gent. London: Printed by Thomas Harper, 1635.

Carter, Edmund. *The History of the University of Cambridge, from Its Origin, to the Year 1753.* London: Cambridge, 1753.

Chalons, Manuel. *The History of France from the Establishment of that Monarchy under Pharamond, to the Death of Lewis XII, Vol. 2.* London: R. Dodsley, 1752.

Chamberlain, George W. *History of Weymouth, Massachusetts in Four Vols., Vol. 3.* Boston: Wright Potter Printing Company, 1923.

Carlisle, Nicholas. *A Concise Description of the Endowed Grammar Schools in England and Wales, Vol. 1.* London: Cradock and Joy, 1818.

Cooke, Edward. *The Second Part of the Institutes of the Laws of England.* London: E.& R. Brooke, 1797.

Coote, Henry C. *The Romans of Britain.* London: Frederic Norgate, 1878.

Currier, John J. *History of Newbury, Mass. 1635–1902.* Boston: Damrell & Upham, 1902.

Davis, William T. *History of the Judiciary of Massachusetts: Including the Plymouth and Massachusetts Colonies, the Province of the Massachusetts Bay, and the Commonwealth.* Boston: Boston Book, Company, 1900.

Dean, John W. *A Memoir of the Rev. Nathaniel Ward.* Albany: J. Munsell, 1868.

Dillaway, C. K. *History of the Grammar School, or the Free School of 1645 in Roxburie.* Roxbury: John Backay, 1860.

Douglass, William. *A Summary, Historical and Political, of the First Planting, Progressive Improvements, and Present State of the British Settlements in North America.* Boston: R. Baldwin, 1755.

Doyle, John A. *English Colonies in America, Vol. 2.* New York: Holt, 1889.

Drake, Samuel G. *Biography and History of the Indians of North America: From Its First Discovery.* Boston: B. B. Mussey, 1851.

Drake, Samuel G———. *History of Middlesex County, Massachusetts*, Boston: Estes and Lauriat Jazzybee Verlaog, 1870.

Drake, Francis S. *The Town of Roxbury: Its Memorable Persons and Places. Its History and Antiquities with Numerous Illustrations of its.* Roxbury: Published By the Author, 1878.

Dyers, G. *History of the University and Colleges of Cambridge: Including Notices of the Founders and Eminent Men, in 2 vols. Vol. 2.* London: Longman, Hurst, Rees, Orme, and Brown, 1814.

Earle, Alice M. *Customs and Fashions in Old New England.* New York: Charles Scribner's Sons, 18949.

Echard, Lauwrence. *The History of England*. London: Jacob Tonson, 1707.

Eliot, Charles W. *The Harvard Classics, Vol. 43*. New York: P.F. Collier & Son, 1910.

Endicott, Charles M. *Memoir of John Endecott, First Governor of the Colony of Massachusetts Bay*. Salem: Printed at the Observer Office, 1847.

Felt, Joseph B. *The Annals of Salem, from Its First Settlement*. Salem: W. & S. B. Ives, 1827.

————Felt, Joseph B. *The Ecclesiastical History of New England, Etc., Vol. 1*. Boston: Congregational Library Association, vol.1, 1855.

Fisher, George W. *Annals of Shrewsbury School*. London: Methuen & Co., 1899.

Frothingham, Richard Jr. *The History of Charlestown, Massachusetts*. Boston: Charles C. Little and James Brown, 1845.

Fowler, William C. *Local Law in Massachusetts and Connecticut, Historically Considered: And The Historical Status of the Negro in Connecticut*. [Albany]:- Joel Munsell, 1872.

Fuller, Oliver P. *The History of Warwick, Rhode Island, from Its Settlement in 1642 to the Present Time*. Providence: Angell, Burlingame & Company, Printers, 1875.

Goldsmith, William. *The Naval History of Great Britain: From the Earliest Period, with Biographical Notices of the Admirals, and Other Distinguished Officers*. London: J. Jacques & Wright, 1825.

Green, John R. *The Making of England, Vol. 1*. London: Macmillan and Co., Limited, 1900.

Green, George W. *A Short History of Rhode Island*. Providence: J. A. & R. A. Reid, Publishers, 1877.

Griffis, William E. *The Pilgrims in their Three Homes: England, Holland, America*. New York: Houghton, Mifflin and Company, 1898.

Grizzell, Emit D. *Origin and Development of the High School in New England before 1865*. New York: The Macmillan Company, 1923.

Guizot, M. *History of the Origin of Representative Government in Europe*. Translated by Andrew R. Scoble. London: Henry G. Bohn, 1861.

Hakluyt, Richard. *Voyages of the Elizabeth Seamen to America: Thirteen Original Narratives, from the Collection of Hakluyt*. London: T. De La Rue & Company, 1880.

Hannay, James. *The History of Acadia, from Its Discovery to its Surrender to England, by the Treaty of Paris*. St. John, N. B.: Printed by J. & A. McMillan, 1879.

Hanson, J. W. *History of the Town of Danvers from Its Early Settlement to the Year 1848*. Danvers:, Published by the Author, 1848.

Hazen, Henry. *History of Billerica, Massachusetts*. Boston: A. Williams and Co., 1883.

Henry, Robert. *The History of Great Britain, Vol. 1*. London: Printed for A. Strahan and T. Cadell Publisher, 1788.

Higginson, Thomas W. *Life of Francis Higginson, First Minister in the Massachusetts Bay Colony, and Author of "New England Plantation."* New York: Dodd, Mead and Company, 1891.

Holmes, Abiel. *The History of Cambridge*. Boston: Samuel Hall, 1801.

Hotten, John C. *The Original Lists of Persons of Quality, Emigrants, Religious Exiles, Political Rebels, Serving Men Sold for a Term of years, Apprentices, Children Stolen, Maidens Pressed, and Others who Went from Great Britain to the American Plantations, 1600–1700*. London: Chatto and Windus, 1874.

Howell, Geo. R. *The Early History of Southampton, L.I. New York, with Genealogies*. New York: J. N. Hollock, 1866.

Hubbard, William. *A General History of New England. Published by the Massachusetts Historical Society*. Cambridge: Hilliard & Metcalf, 1815.

Hume, David. *The History of the Reign of Henry the Eighth: Written by David Hume, Vol. 2*. London: D. Brewman, 1792.

Hunt, William. *Bristol*. London: Longmans, Green, and Co. 1887.

Hutchinson, Thomas. *The History of Massachusetts*. Salem: Thomas C. Cushing, 1795.

Jackson, Francis. *History of the Early Settlement of Newton, County of Middlesex, Massachusetts from 1639 to 1800*. Boston: Stacy and Richardson, 1854.

Johnson, Richard. *A New History of England from the Earlier Period to the Present Time. On a File Recommended by the Earl of Chesterfield, etc.* London: Printed for F. Newbery, 1775.

Josselyn, John. *Account of Two Voyages to New England*. London: Giles Widdowees, 1674.

Julius Caesar, *C. Julius Caesar's Commentaries on the Gaul War*. Boston: Crocker and Brewster, 1864.

Lambert, Edward R. *History of the Colony of New Haven*. New Haven: Hitchcock & Stafford, 1839.

Leach, Arthur F. *The Schools of Medieval England*. New York: The Macmillan Company, 1915.

Lewis, Alonzo. *The History of Lynn, Including Nahant*. Boston: Samuel N. Dickson, 1844.

Lincoln, Solomon, Jr. *History of the Town of Hingham, Plymouth County, Massachusetts*. Hingham: C. Gill, Jr: Farmer and Brown, 1827.

Lyman, Rollo La Verne. *English Grammar in American Schools Before 1850*. The University of Chicago Libraries. Reprint from Department of the Interior, Bureau of Education, *Bulletin*, 1921, No. 12, 1921, 1922.

Mauduit, Israel. *A Short View of the History of the Colony of Massachusetts Bay: With Respect to Their Charters and Constitution*. London: J. Wilkie, 1774.

Moore, Jacob B. *Lives of the Governors of New Plymouth and Massachusetts Bay*. New York: Gates & Stedman, 1848.

Moore, Walter. *Boston (Lincolnshire) and Its Surroundings: With an Account of the Pilgrim Fathers of New England*. London: Homeland Association, 1908.

Murray, Hugh. *Historical Account of Discovery and Travels in America*. London: Longman, Rees, Orne, Brown, & Green, 1829.

Otis, James. Ruth of Boston: A Story of the Massachusetts Bay Colony. New York: American Book Company, 1910.

Paige, Lucius R. *History of Cambridge, Massachusetts*. Boston: H. O. Houghton Company Press, 1877.

Palgrave, Sir Francis Sir. *History of the Anglo-Saxons*. London: John Murray, 1831.

Parker, James. *The Early History of Oxford 727–1100. Preceded by a Sketch of the Mythical Origin of the City and University*. Oxford: Printed for the Oxford Historical Society at the Clarendon Press, 1885.

Peirce, Benjamin. *A History of Harvard University: From Its Foundation in the Year 1636, to the Period of the American Revolution*. Cambridge: Brown, Shattluck, and Company, 1833.

Prichard, S. J. *The Town and City of Waterbury, Connecticut, Vol. 1*. New Haven: The Price & Lee Company, 1896.

Quincy, Josiah. *The History of Harvard University, Vol. 1*. Cambridge: John Owen, 1840.

Reeves, John. *History of the English Law, from the Time of the Saxons, to the End of the Reign of Elizabeth, Vol. 5*. London: Printed by A. Strahans, 1829.

Robert, Oliver A. *History of the Military Company of the Massachusetts, Now Called The Ancient and Honorable Artillery, Vol. 1*. Boston: Alfred Mudge & Son, Printers, 1895.

Roberts, George. *The Social History of the People of the Southern Counties of England in Past Centuries*. London: Longman, Brown, Green & Robert, 1856.

Ruggles, Thomas. *The History of Poor: Their Rights, Duties, and The Laws Respecting Them. In a Series of Letters*. London: W. Richardson, 1797.

Smith, Charles J. *Autographs of Royal, Noble, Learned and Remarkable Personages Conspicuous in English History*. London: Printed by and for J.B. Nichols and Son, 1829.

Smith, S. F. *History of Newton, Massachusetts Town and City from Its Earliest Settlement to the Present Time 1630–1880*. Boston: The American Logotype Company, 1880.

Snow, Caleb H. *A History of Boston: The Metropolis of Massachusetts, from Its Origin to the Present; with some Account of the Environs*. Boston: A. Bowen, 1828.

Spencer, George W. *A New, Authentic, and Complete History of England, from the First Settlement of Brutus in this Island, Upwards of A Thousand Years before the Time of Julius Caesar, to the Year 1795*. London: Printed for the Author, sold by Alex. Hogg, 1794.

Strype, John. *The Life of the Learned Sir John Cheke, Knight. First Instructor, Afterwards Secretary of State to King Edward VI*. Oxford: at the Clarendon Press, 1821.

Suzzallo, Henry. *The Rise of Local School Supervision in Massachusetts (The School Committee, 1635–1827)*. New York: Published by Teachers College, Columbia University, 1906.

Tacitus, Cornelius. *The Works of Tacitus. The Oxford Translation, Revised with Notes, Vol. ,2. The History, Germany, Agricola, and Dialogue on Orators*. London: George Bell & Sons, 1889.

Thayer, William R. *An Historical Sketch of Harvard University, from Its Foundation to May, 1890*. Cambridge, Massachusetts:[? Publisher not identified, 1890.

Thompson, Benjamin F. *History of Long Island: Containing Account of the Discovery and Settlement*. New York: E. French, 1839.

Tindal, N. *The History of England Written in French by Mr. Rapin de Thoyras. Translated into English, with Additional Notes, Vol.1*. London: Printed for John and Paul Knapton, 1743.

Toland, John. *A Critical History of the Celtic Religion, and Learning: Containing an Account of the Druids; Or, the Priest and Judges*. Edinburgh: Printed by John Findlay,, 1815.

Trail, H. J. *Social England A Record of the Progress of the People*. New York: G. P. Putnam's Sons, 1898.

Trumbull, Hammond J. *The Memorial History of Hartford County Connecticut 1633–1884 in 2 Vols*. Boston: Edward L. Osgood Publisher, 1886.

Turner, Sharon. *The History of The Anglo-Saxons from the Earliest Period to the Norman Conquest, Vol. 1*. Paris: Baudry's European Library, 1840.

Tyler, Lyon G. *Narratives of Early Virginia, 1606–1625, Vol. 5*. New York: C. Scribner's Sons, 1907.

Waters, Thomas F. *Ipswich In the Massachusetts Bay Colony. A History of the Town from 1700 to 1917.* Ipswich: The Ipswich Historical Society,. Ipswich, 1917.

Washburn, Emory. *Sketches of the Judicial History of Massachusetts from 1630 to the Revolution in 1775.* Boston: Charles C. Little and James Brown, 1840.

Webster, Noah. *History of the United States: To Which is Prefixed. A Brief Historical Account of Our [English] Ancestors.* New York: S. Bobcock, 1837.

Whitekar, Epher. *Southold, 1640–1740. History of Southold, L.I. Its First Century.* Southold: Printed for the Author, 1881.

Winthrop, John and James Kendal Hosmer. *Winthrop's Journal "History of New England," 1630–1649, Vol. 1.* New York: Charles Scribner's Sons, 1908.

Winthrop, John. *The History of New England from 1630 to 1649, Vol. 2.* Boston: Printed by Thomas E. Wait and Son, helps and Farnham, 1826.

Walcott, Charles H. *Concord in the Colonial Period:. Being a History of the Town of Concord, Massachusetts, 1635–1689.* Boston: Estes and Lauriat, 1884

Wright, Thomas. *Anglo-Saxon Period.* London: J. W. Parker, 1842.

Zimmermann, Wilhelm. *A Popular History of Germany: From the Earliest Period to the Present Day, Vol. 1.* New York: H. J. Johnson, 1897.

Index